Diari

Ex-Adult Entertainer: My Road to Redemption

This is My Life, My Journey, My Story, My Testimony

An Autobiography

Robyn Robbins

Diaries of an Ex-Adult Entertainer

Written by: Robyn Robbins

Cover by The Authors Help Desk TM

Editing & Formatting by The Authors Help Desk TM

Mail To:

Robyn Robbins Enterprises LLC

P.O. Box 476 Norcross Ga, 30091

ISBN: 1494426110
ISBN-13: 978-1494426118

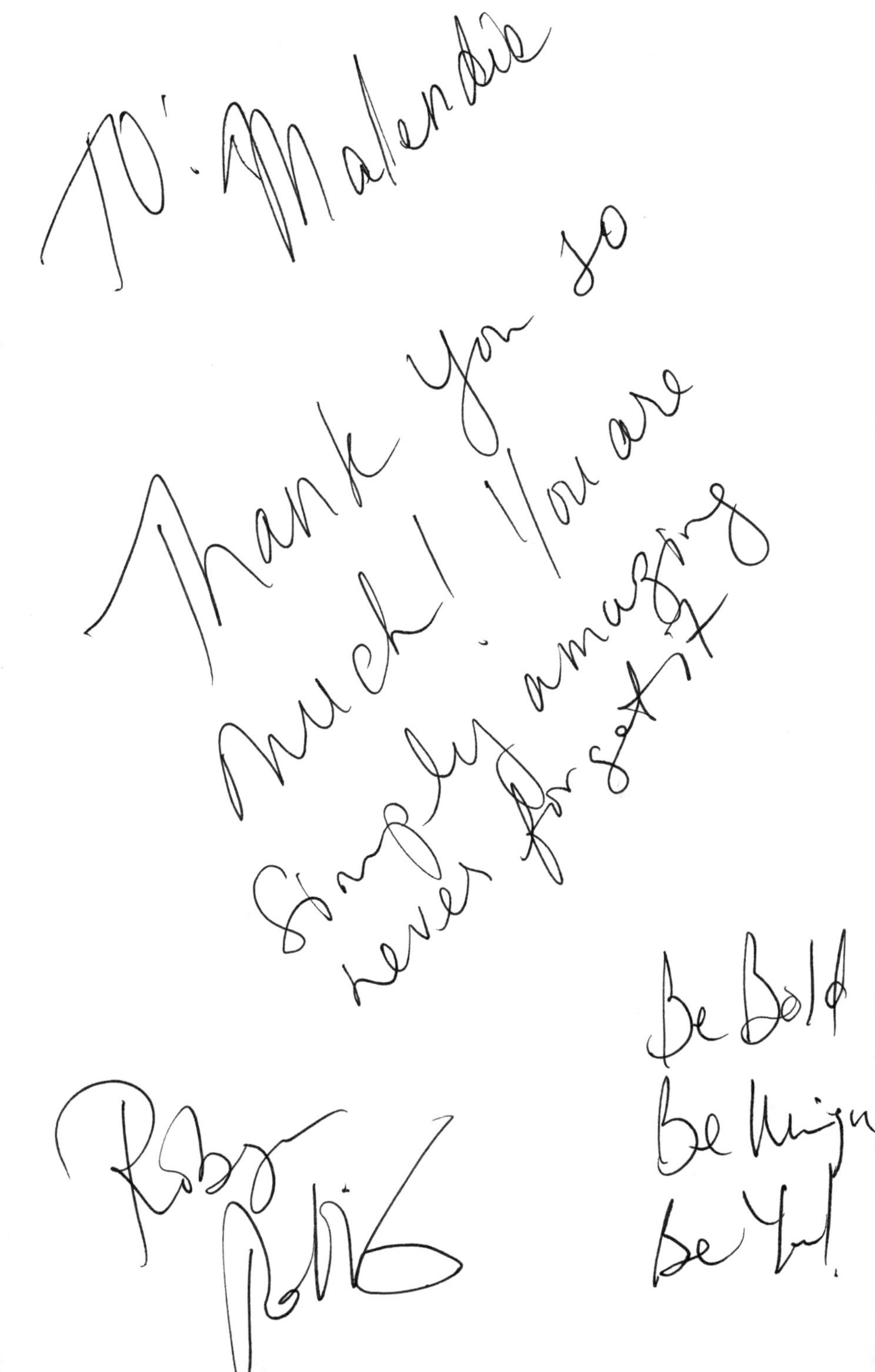

Other Books By Robyn Robbins

“The Refocus Challenge: A 40 Day Personal Training Guide To Refocus. Revamp. Revitalize YOU”

“Esther’s Oil: The Anointing of Esther “Volume 1 Edition 2 Training System

Coming soon:

“Daddy’s Little Girls: Daughters of God”

“Are They All DEAD Yet?”

“The Way: Principals and Keys for Kingdom Servants”

DEDICATIONS

I honor my Lord and Savior Jesus Christ, not only with this book but with my life! I love you and thank you for being everything to me. Thank you for never giving up on me even when I gave up on myself. Thank you for keeping me through all of it. Thank you for not allowing my poor choices to define my future and my destiny!

I dedicate this book to the ministry of Bishop O.C Allen. I am grateful to the ministry the Lord has given you as it has helped to change my life!

I dedicate this book to my deceased biological parents. I made it! See how good God is! I also dedicate this book to anyone who feels broken, bitter at life, alone, abandoned, abused, betrayed, rejected, neglected, and those who feel simply forgotten.

I dedicate this book to that broken little girl who feels as though she is destined for a horrible, unfulfilling life.

I dedicate this book to that person who feels as though God doesn't want you or love you because of who you are. What you have gone through will make you stronger and wiser. Although it may feel at times like it is going to *kill you*, know that God has a different plan for your life!

I dedicate this book to every woman and man in the clutches of adult entertainment. What you do or did for a living is neither who you are nor what God created you to be!

It took a lot to write this book as I am a private person. I suffered with fear and toiled so many times because I didn't want to experience some of the ridicule that this book will bring! However I realized your freedom and or empowerment is more IMPORTANT than my temporary discomfort!

It is my prayer that you clearly see that healing and freedom are both real! They are as real as the one who created and releases it. God is real, alive and loves us unconditionally! He desires for us to be whole and walk in our authentic selves, purpose, destiny and in authority as he predestined for us.

Contents

PREFACE

Can you imagine someone asking you to share your deepest intimate secrets with the world? The secrets that may raise eyebrows and cause others to judge and gossip about you, the secrets that are shameful, the ones you are not proud of the ones you keep buried and hidden away. That's the feeling I had when I received the directive to write this book.

I had absolutely no desire to tell my secrets in fact I had never stood up to testify at a testimony service. My testimony was to stay between God, myself, those who were there to witness it and the few I had deemed trustworthy to share pieces of it. I struggled and toiled with the Lord taking me a little over 3 yrs to finish this book!

While writing this book I was forced to relive and or face certain experiences or things. I would weep for the broken little girl and the confused vengeful adolescent I was then. Weeping for them freed me all the more. The places where I thought I was completely healed but realized I wasn't got healed during the process.

I was so worried about people that this book almost didn't make it and once it was finished I still had a shadow of fear lingering around.

The first run of this book was purchased by family, friends and those that desired to show support. I received great feedback from everyone however there were a handful of individuals that said “I can tell that you held back in the book”. The truth I said is that I wanted to use wisdom as I wrote the book and I didn’t want to come off as bashing those who have hurt me because I’m passed that. I wanted to be careful and use tact. Plus if I wrote every little thing I would still be writing, I am still alive I laughed. Maybe I was even protecting myself in away, hoping I didn’t make myself look to bad but the truth is it was bad and I was a complete mess! No need to cover up now right, go figure.

Their response was “so you are protecting them and yourself? What you with hold will affect the impact that this book could have he warned. What did God ask you to do? He asked. To give the raw uncut truth I replied, those were the words exactly! Have you done that? He responded. I thought I did but I guess not and here we are. I realized sometimes when you receive a directive it seems if you do it to some extent you have obeyed. The truth is that half way doing what you have been told is still considered disobedience. So I decided to go back and ask God to lead me so the full purpose of this book may be fulfilled. I promised that I wouldn’t with hold out of fear, shame or the opinions of others. I am so grateful to those that God has placed in my life to hold me accountable. Thank You!

Introduction

I want to take this opportunity to prepare you for what you're about to read. This book might be explicit at times because it is the raw uncut TRUTH. The name of all establishments and parties has been changed in order to protect their privacy. My desire is to simply give my testimony and for God to get the Glory. I want him to have his way in whatever way he sees fit.

Please know that the views, thoughts and ways I once had as it pertains to men while I was in the adult entertainment industry are not the views, thoughts and ways I have today! It was important to let you (the reader) completely in so that you can have an understanding of where I was at that time in my life.

This book was not written to change you're theology nor to debate scripture; I wrote this book in obedience to the Holy Spirit because it is the desire of God to expose the enemy! Many go into adult entertainment and the sex industry thinking that it's harmless but it's a door you would never open if you knew the truth. What seems glamorous and a quick way out is a trick of deception and ploy to kill the soul and spirit of the victim.

If you have purchased this book then you know that I was in adult entertainment and that God has delivered me from that life. I pray that whatever it is that God wants to give you or do in you through reading this book that it is accomplished in Jesus's name: **Amen!**

I would have never thought in a million years that God would choose someone like me.

"[No] for God selected (deliberately chose) what in the world is foolish to put the wise to shame, and what the world calls weak to put the strong to shame."

~ 1 Corinthians 1:27

Please be sure to read the ***adult entertainment definitions*** so that you are able to understand the terms used in this book. As you proceed through this book, do so with an open heart! Blessings

Adult Entertainment Definitions

Sissification: A training used in BDSM that trains the submissive to take on feminine roles and even feminine features by the dominant partner, a popular form of humiliation.

Humiliation: One psychological technique a Dominate may use. The methods used may be verbal or physical.

Brown showers: To receive the bowels of another person on your body parts, usually the dominant. This is a practice known in the BDSM community as an act of humiliation.

Golden showers: To receive the urine of another person on your body parts, usually the dominant. This is a practice known in the BDSM community as an act of humiliation

BDSM: Bondage, Discipline, Dominance, Submission, Sadism and Masochism

Animal Play: To be referred to as the human pet as a form of humiliation and a practice in BDSM. The sub is made to act like the animal of choice. Most common role plays are dogs and cats.

Pay pig: A submissive that consents to financial domination from the Mistress or Dom/Master.

Fetish: A sexual fixation on non-sexual objects or items.

Role play: To act and speak as the character you are portraying.

Dominatrix: A woman who practices BDSM daily – either professionally or in her personal life. She controls a submissive mentally, physically and financially by using their femininity.

Escort/VIP Courtesan: One who is paid by the hour, not the act. However, sexual activity is usually involved.

Sensual Body Rub Artist: One who performs body work in a sensual way using light strokes and feathering techniques. Body work usually ends with a sexual release

Professional Swinger: One who dates/sleeps with multiple people for pay.

Trick or John: is a term used for a person that spends money for services (usually sexual acts, fetishes or companionship)

CHAPTER 1

In The Beginning

I was born on the cold day of February 19, 1987 in Bronx, New York to my beloved parents. I was the fourth child so I had 3 older sisters. From what I can remember about my short lived childhood, I had an artistic musical family. My mother's voice was beautiful. My oldest sister sang, designed clothes and drew cartoon characters. She was really good! That creative gene skipped the second oldest completely but she is very smart and responsible (she's the one with several degrees and certificates). My third oldest sister sang every chance she got! They would sing around the house – their voices like angels!

I was christened (baby dedication) as my parents were believers who were so caught up in life that the practical application seemed as though it would never be tangible. I remember the time when we went to church as a family and my uncle played those drums as though his life depended on it! We chuckled at the faces he made.

My parents loved to host and cook; they were great at it! They loved to have a good time. Sometimes they argued and fought but I don't remember it being too often. My parents both worked multiple jobs to care for us. Some would say we were disciplined harshly and that it was abuse. I can't argue that. My parents did the only thing they knew. My mom came from an abusive broken home as well.

I remember specifically getting a beaten because I cut the wire off the radio. Sparks flew and the bed almost caught fire. I slid under the bed in fear. My sister Tammy told Mom what I had done. I remember mom taking my clothes off, wetting my body in the tub and then standing me on the coffee table to beat me with an extension cord. I don't think I ever misbehaved after that.

I remember lots of laughter, joy, pain and parties. There was always a party to go to, either a family member or one of our friends' birthday. That's where I found out that I had my very own musical gift. I could move my body in such a gifted way to music. I was the hype of the party:

"Look at that little girl dance," is how they would express their astonishment that a little girl could move so well.

I began moving to music ever since I could walk but really starting emulating what I saw at 3-years-old. I remember the feeling I would get when I danced. It was complete joy and the attention that came with it wasn't bad either.

There was one particular party when our favorite reggae song came on. At that time, there was a dance move called the spider. I put my feet on the wall, hands on the ground and began to pop my lower half on the wall. My older sisters had to convince the people that I was only 5-years-old because they assumed I was a little older!

My siblings and I used to be close before our Mom passed away.

We went to the pool in the summer and loved to go skating. My older sisters probably hated that I had to go everywhere with them but they loved me. I remember mommy saying "Always take care of each other first before you help someone else!"

In New York, skating and dancing were a way of life. My sisters would be skating in the large rink and I would go to the second rink and watch them dance and battle. My sisters always found me in the middle of the crowd dancing.

Before my mother passed away, my childhood had more happy memories than painful ones. The first really painful one for me was when my father became addicted to drugs. He was a correction officer when he suffered from a really bad accident on the job. The doctors had to prescribe a controlled substance for pain and that's how he became an addict.

After that he was no longer daddy. He went from fully functional to unrecognizable. We barely saw him in the beginning but then we didn't see him any because my mom kicked him out for stealing our toys and stuff to sell for drugs. I had officially lost my Dad. His absence in my life was unbearable. What's said is that I didn't realize just how much I missed and needed him.

The second painful memory from my childhood was when Tammy and I got molested by our mom's new boyfriend. It was mid-afternoon as Tammy napped on the couch. She was wearing white shorts and a tan stripped top. I was supposed to be sleeping as well but for some reason I couldn't. The house was so quiet. The only sound was the fan blowing in the living room where Tammy was resting. I quietly walked to the kitchen anticipating a snack. I walked light, trying not to wake anyone.

I didn't understand what I saw as I crouched down in between the two pillars where there was an opening in the kitchen. I watched as he rubbed her bottom and slip his hands in her shorts. She woke up crying hysterically. Not long after the incident with my sister, he brought me to the kitchen and said that he would fix me something to eat. He pulled out his private part and asked me to touch *it*. He assured me that it was okay. After a while, he made "*white stuff* "come out and told me to taste it. I remember instantly feeling sick. It was like I had consumed a whole bunch of salt!

I began to cry and he began to comfort me and ask if I wanted candy. He offered me a bunch of things until I was completely calm.

The last painful memory was the death of my beautiful mother. I remember my mom throwing up chunks and lots of blood in the toilet. I remember rubbing her head saying, "Mommy it's going to be okay."

My mom was hospitalized so I didn't see her much. She had a hyper active thyroid, which caused major complications. She had a massive heart attack. The last time I saw my mother, she was lying in the casket. I was told by Tammy to say good bye to Mommy and I did.

My childhood ended at the age of six! I had to grow up fast and I was never the same again!!

CHAPTER 2

Innocence

What if I said that I've held a position in almost every area of the adult entertainment industry except porn? What if I told you that I have been a sex phone operator, an exotic dancer, a V.I.P courtesan (Upscale escort), a dominatrix, a fetish/role play escort, a sensual body rub artist, a professional swinger and that I ran my own agency that offered almost everything listed above? Would you believe me?

Well it is the raw, uncut truth! When I got into this industry, it was simply to survive and to create a better life for myself and my loved ones. I quickly discovered that adult entertainment is a world of its own. Why I ended up there didn't matter. After about six to seven months, the industry completely changed me.

I became entrenched in the jaws of that world so much that it held me captive. No matter what I tried to do, it seemed like I just couldn't escape! Let's look at how this all came to be.

Innocence? That was lost when I was molested at the age of six. Although he didn't rape me, he had exposed me to things and forced me to commit acts that will forever be vividly embedded in my mind. I remember watching the same man molest my older sister as she napped on the living room couch. She slept; unaware of what was taking place as he touched her in her secret places. This man selfishly indulged in his own fleshly desires, not caring about the damage he would cause to two little girls who had a destiny. This man would go on to father my little sister and brother.

This was the first of many incidents in my life where I would be violated. Due to us being sexually violated we were taken from our mother and put in the foster care system. Mommy worked so hard to get us back. She did everything requested of her. It seemed like we were back for only a short period of time before mom got really sick. There were times when I would go to her room and knock for about four minutes. I wouldn't hear a sound so I would barge into the room. Sometimes it looked like mom was dead in the bed. Her body was lifelessly limp and positioned in ways that I can't explain. In addition to my mother's condition, I believe she died of a broken heart as well. Not too long after our mother's death, we were all put in the Foster Care system for a second time.

I felt hurt and unwanted. I couldn't understand why no family member would take us, not even our own father. I guess getting his next fix was more important than his own children at the time. The Foster Care system split us up: the eldest and her children lived with our God parents. My two older sisters (Sasha and Tammy) ended up in one home and the four of us (Tia, Sharday, Kareem and I) ended up in another.

We bounced from place to place because I wouldn't allow the foster parents to care for my siblings. I would throw fits and tantrums until they got the picture: I was the one who would change their diapers and feed them! No one else could touch them unless I felt they were alright. For a while my siblings addressed me as mommy, a habit they soon would be broken out of by our adoptive mother Raven. She despised the way they addressed me. No one understood the bond my siblings and I had developed, while hard to explain I can at least describe it. We have a bond of protection, trust, love, loyalty and this unspoken innate feeling of we are all we have.

My Uncle C and his wife Aunt Shelly came and got us. They had a big house in Queens. Aunt Shelly's mother and sister owned the house so they also lived there. Auntie Shelly had two sons of her own so we had others to play with. We were happy and felt safe. Then my uncle started to snap because he couldn't handle the death of his only sister, our mother.

He would get angry and beat me while screaming, "You killed her! It's your fault my sister is dead!" Then he slammed me into the floor, picked me up and threw me under the desk. My sisters and brother were all crying! When auntie and her mom heard the commotion, they came upstairs and got him off of me!! They kicked him out to protect us but auntie couldn't care for all six kids by herself so we went back into foster care. I remember the day we left; we loaded our belongings in this big navy blue van. Auntie Shelly sister Raven promised us she would get us back.

We stayed with this Spanish lady who seemed to be alright but it was very clear that she fancied our little brother more than us. Everything was about him so much so that she often forgot about the rest of us. Due to her neglect, my sister Shardae suffered from thrash several times.

The next home we were in was with an African-American family in Brooklyn. We called the foster Mother SweePea. SweePea had one biological daughter, Nicole, who also lived with her. That home seemed alright until the punishments began. I remember specifically not getting the best report from school one day. I didn't know what it was called at the time, but I was basically depressed and there was no participation on my part. I would often fall asleep in class due to the depression.

SweePea made me stand in the corner all night long without dinner after my homework was done. I wasn't sure if she forgot about me or if it was intentional. I remember waking up on the floor to a wooden paddle because I wasn't standing up and had fallen asleep. My sister Shardae was a very sensitive and nervous person. One day, SweePea began to yell at her. She got so scared and nervous that she vomited.

SweePea went to get the paddle. I begged SweePea not to beat her. I was explaining to her that when my sister got scared, she vomited. SweePea made me clean up the mess and then told me to beat her or else she would beat me worst. I pleaded with her to forgive my sister but she didn't care. I struck my sister and she screamed, SweePea and Nicole laughed uncontrollably at my sister's reaction.

I must have blacked out because I don't remember being present after the second hit. All I remember was rage filling my heart and when I came out of it, Shardae was lying on the floor balled up with no voice to neither cry nor scream. My little sister's bottom and legs were black and blue. What just happened? I couldn't make since of it.

I helped my sister up off the floor as best as I could, crying uncontrollably while whimpering the words, "I'm sorry, I'm so sorry. Please forgive me." I held my baby sister in the bed and we both cried until we fell asleep. I hated myself! The word *hate* can't describe what I felt for myself that day! We were so glad when we left that home!

I remember us coming to a home that looked like something out of a fairy tale book (in my child like mind) and I felt we were safe. However, this home would turn into a living nightmare! We were disciplined harshly – so harshly that I would lie and say it was my fault to save them from the abuse that would follow. I never wanted to see my siblings get punished again after what happened in the previous home. The punishment varied depending on what we did. If it was a minor infraction, we would scrub the bathroom floor with a tooth brush. If it was something worst then our Foster Mother would put rice down in a corner and have us kneel on it until our knees bled. The worst punishment was to be punished by her husband (a tall dark skinned heavyset man) who all the children called Papa.

I remember enduring those punishments like it was yesterday. I specifically remember our foster mother saying to me "I'm going to let Papa handle you this evening!"

I remember her giving me a bath and sending me into the room where he was waiting. He rose up and said, "So I heard that you were horrible today. Do you know what happens to little girls with extremely horrible behavior?"

I replied "No" while shaking with fear. He had me take off my pajamas and whipped me with a belt and the belt buckle. Once he tired out, he said, "Now what are you going to do to make this right?" He then dropped his pants and began to *instruct* me.

This would take place during the rest of our time there, even when I didn't do anything wrong. I remember how I used to shake in fear when I would smell his scent in the air.

Finally, Auntie Raven made good on her promise and got us back. She began the process of adoption not too long after. We were happy children since they were Christians and were very active in the church. We went to church, bible school, sang on the choir, danced on the dance ministry, joined the girl scouts and every summer went to a two-week Christian sleep away camp.

When we got disciplined, it was normal discipline – nothing abusive. We were happy and grateful. We had great birthdays and an awesome Christmas every year. For the first time in a long time, we felt safe. Unfortunately, that atmosphere would be short lived. Our Aunt Raven (aunt by marriage/Adoptive Mother) began to date a man, who unknown to us was the *"spawn of Satan"* himself. At that point, everything began to change.

At first, we really liked him because he would help plead our case so that she would loosen the reins up a bit and he made fun suggestions on our behalf. We were being brought up in a strict Pentecostal /Holiness Christian home. For example: we were not allowed to spend the night out nor have friends spent the night in.

They barely could come over because they would say spirits transferred. For us to have a friend outside of family members meant they had to meet the parents as well as the friend to feel comfortable and that rarely happened.

Dan would take us to the park and the beach in the summer. We all really felt like he was the dad we never had. As time went on, we began to see his true nature surface whenever he would drink or become really angry. He would yell at us, go into a rage, beat us and do the same to our Aunt, who we already called "Mom."

When I was 12-years-old, I had the weirdest dream. One night as we got ready for bed, something felt different but I couldn't put my figure on it. As a child, I dreamed a lot and those dreams felt so incredibly real.

I laid down on my pillow and looked around until I fell to sleep. I saw three mummies lying in my bed. Two of their faces were unraveled, one was my biological mother and the other was my dear Grammy. The third face was wrapped but the mouth was open and an invisible hand with pliers pulled the teeth out one by one.

When I woke up, it was a calm rested on me. I didn't understand what I was feeling; although that wasn't the first time something like this had happened to me. It felt like I was prepared for it.

About 2 weeks passed and Mom called us all in her room. She looked worried. She said to us "I'm not sure how to say this to you all. God please give me strength!"

Then I said "It's okay Mommy. Gee Gee is dead, right?"

Mom looked at me in shock and broke down, shaking her head yes and my siblings began to cry. I had that same calm on me that I had when I woke up from the dream. Gee Gee was our oldest sister and we had lost her. It was this dream that made me realize I wasn't just dreaming nor having nightmares. There was something more to it. A few months later Gee Gee's newborn son died as well. What was devastating to our family was that Gee Gee died from bacteria in her blood. We couldn't understand why this wasn't detected during her pregnancy with all the monthly routine testing that they do.

The second devastating thing was that it was her children who discovered her body as she passed away in her sleep. They were in the house with our sister for about a day or two when they realized something was wrong. Gee Gee oldest son tried to get help from the neighbors but no one was home and so he called 911. I can't imagine the trauma our niece and nephews had gone through especially the newborn.

I remember all of us traveling down south for her funeral. My older sisters talked about how hard it was to bury her and how upset they were that we weren't able to have a head stone for Gee Gee. They were upset because it happened again as Mom didn't have a head stone either. Another major loss for our family the pain we felt was unbearable.

In the summer of that year (1999), Dan had us bring our sleeping bags to our mother's room.

He said, "Let's watch a movie. You can all make a palate on the floor with your sleeping bags and pillows."

It was a movie that we had all been dying to see, *'Deep Blue Sea'*. So we did as he said and made our palates on the floor. Of course, as children we did fall asleep during the movie.

When I woke up, I was no longer on the floor but in my Mothers bed with her boyfriend in between my legs. I was screaming, crying and hitting him so that he would get off me. Everyone was gone. I wondered why no one could hear me and why they wouldn't help me. I felt completely helpless! All he kept saying was how sorry he was and how it's okay. He told me that I had nothing to worry about. He even promised that he would take me to the store and that I could buy whatever I wanted. Come to find out my siblings were playing outside with friends while this was going on.

As we were all loading the car, he said to me, "Don't worry, you haven't done anything wrong. It's natural. This is what Dad's do with daughters who are special like you so don't feel bad." His words didn't stop me from feeling helpless and confused. I was only 12 years old and my life was about to take yet another turn, a turn that would change not only my life but my sight. This would be the seed that served as a foundation for the things to come.

In the beginning of this he would call me into the room and when I got there he would have porn playing on the TV. He would have me sit on the bed and watch it with him. After a while he would ask me how I felt and if I wanted what the woman was getting on TV? At the time I couldn't make since of what was happening to my body. Of course now I know it was arousal that I was experiencing. I would just say my body felt funny and asked if he could put his mouth on my private area like on the T.V. As time went on it happened over and over again.

I would go on to eventually lose my virginity to Dan and become his *play thing* for the next 4 years. What's sad is that I believed everything he told me. I mean it made sense. It had happened so many times before that I really did think it was normal. He would come to me at night while Tia and I slept and would mess with me while I slept. He would summon me if I was home from school during the day. He did what he wanted when he wanted. I had no say in it, I was numb to it and I was a slave to it. It was like I became addicted to the feeling of physical release and High.

One time Dan snuck one of his baby mamas into the house. They went upstairs in the room (the bedroom that Dan and Mom shared).We was all down stairs playing around when we should have been doing homework. Dan called me from the upstairs room. I ran upstairs "yes" I said. Immediately hushed and shocked at what I was seeing, I saw her lying in the bed naked with a sheet draped across her. Her legs open in the same position that you often would see when a woman is giving birth. Dan was naked on his knees motioning me with his hand to come toward him. I quietly closed and locked the door. I came over and got on my knees and watched. He was performing oral and fingering acts on her while she moaned in pleasure. I became aroused at what I saw and took off my bottoms. It was just like watching what we always watched on TV.

After a while he motioned me again. I came closer and he pointed to her private area suggesting that it was my turn. So I did what he suggested. He quickly laid underneath me and began to perform oral on my private area. After about three minutes she sat up and began to scream at Dan."What the hell is going on, what do you have her in here for, what the hell is wrong with you?!"

He tried to calm her down and began to sweet talk her. I tried to calm her down telling her that it was okay, really it was I said. I was confused- highly aroused but secretly relieved and then I ran downstairs! A little later on that Day he tried to teach her how to drive I guess to appease her and totaled the green van Mom had just purchased.

Being used to this, I began to go to him on my own at times. I would go to him when I thought he was mad at me or just mad period to make him happy and calm. It's crazy how he made me feel accepted and loved.

He had a side to him, a crazy wild streak. He was another person when he was like that. It was like Dr. Jekyll and Mr. Hyde. For us there were moments when he actually acted like a father (Dr. Jekyll) and then there was the angry, destructive, abusive, sex crazed drug addict (Mr. Hyde).

I watched this man abuse everything that I loved. He would beat my mother senseless time and time again. My siblings and I would jump in to defend our mother but he would begin to beat on us. Mom would just stand there crying and screaming while her children were pummeled by his fist and trampled by his feet. She never dared to step in and save us. Still to this day I am not sure if she was in shock or what it was that paralyzed her in those moments. All I know is that everything Dan touched, he tried to completely destroy!

One day I got the notation to use what he wanted from me to get my way. When I did and it worked, I quickly realized the *"power"* in sex. When I discovered that power, I felt like I had a fighting chance. I had finally felt like I had some form of control over my body, but little did I know that I wouldn't for quite some time.

Around that time in my life, Dan's father would have me to perform sexual favors on him in exchange for money. For the next two years this would happen.

No matter where I went, some guy desired me. If I didn't want to give it willingly, it was taken from me! Like the day we visited Dan's Fathers church where he was an active Deacon. I made a mental vow on that day as he took me forcefully in the basement of his church that I will be in control and I would call the shots. I would say when, where, and even how! Where was God? Did God not like me? What was wrong with me? I was desolate, voided of self, joy and love yet filled with such anger!

I began to hate these men and wanted nothing more than to destroy them the way that they destroyed me!

I went through that for quite some time. I was abused emotionally, mentally, physically and sexually by my mom's husband. I was beat with my mother's husband's fists, bat, gun, boards, thrown down stairs, held at gun point and even locked in the basement of the house for days at a time. My mom was a work-a-holic, she had to be in order to provide for us. Dan didn't work and couldn't keep a job. The sad truth is that she didn't mind the way he disciplined us, she was in total agreement she would say things like "that's what you get". There were even times that she laughed while he beat us. The worst of them all was how she with held food from us and other necessities as well. Yes food, she would store and lock it up in her room. I remember saying to myself and my sister Tia that I couldn't wait to turn 14 yrs old just so I could start working. She was neglectful, emotionally and verbally abusive as well.

It was when he held me at gun point in the basement of our house that I realized he was on way more than alcohol. He pulled out a silver and brown gun from an olive colored duffle bag next to my room in the basement.

The gun tip was sawed off; it looked something like a shot gun. He would tell me how he couldn't help himself because he loved me so much. He began to wave the gun around as he raved about how Raven couldn't stand me because she was jealous of my beauty and how he felt about me. He began to talk about wanting her to die because all he wanted was the money he would get from her insurance. I remember feeling sick as tears rolled down my face. I remembered thinking *please just pull the trigger!*

Witnessing my siblings being abused physically, mentally, emotionally and endure neglect caused me to snap. I couldn't take any more! The gruesome beatings, the horrible mistreatment and the neglect were too much to handle. I just couldn't stomach it anymore! I had been in trouble off and on at school throughout this time. I had no respect for my adoptive Mother Raven. I was angry and enraged. My adoptive mother knew what her husband was doing to me, yet she didn't protect me or my siblings. She clearly chose her husband over us.

One night while my sister and I were sleeping, he came downstairs in the middle of the night (as he often did). After a while, Raven came to the top of the basement steps and began to yell "Dan! What are you doing down there? Come upstairs!"

The yelling was piercing and woke me up. Still to this day, I ask myself why she didn't just come down the stairs. It was so bad that I would sleep through him messing with me (I slept heavier because of the medication I was on)I realized he had visit me when I woke up and felt all of what I thought at the time was abnormal moisture in my private area.

Finally I got up the courage to speak out and tell my mother about her abusive husband. She didn't believe me and told me that if it did happen then it was my fault. Why would I wait so long to say anything? She also said that I was fast and I was just *asking for it* by the way I dressed around the house."

That crushed me in a way that words could never describe how I felt. I believed her – I believed that it was my fault. It was something I couldn't escape no matter where I went so it had to be. I believed that it was supposed to be that way. She had to be right. I mean I would go to him sometimes and I even enjoyed it at times as well.

As a result of my forth-coming and behavior, I was placed in a mental institution for evaluation. The first time was when I was 13-years-old when I stayed for 2 to 3 months. The second time I was the age of 14-years-old. I stayed for six months. The last time I was in a mental institution was when I was about 15-years-old and stayed for about 2 months. I was diagnosed with bipolar disorder at that time. I later find out as an adult that I was misdiagnosed, that I really had PTSD (Post traumatic stress disorder).

I believe she put me in the hospital to cover up what was happening in that house. She didn't want the church or the community to find out. What would they think of her if they did?

Maybe I was going crazy? How was I supposed to handle all of this? Who was going to help me make since and cope with it? My behaviors were a silent cry for help since talking never got me very far. It got me an open investigation by a social worker in which my siblings were forced to lie and I was manipulated to say that I lied and to take it back. That way Raven could have her family the way she wanted it.

Plus she didn't want the embarrassment from those issues to ruin the picture perfect family that she had created so she put me in the hospital as a cover up so she could say with a clear conscience "My daughter is not well. She has problems!"

Secondly, not having a voice was just the icing on the cake. Something inside of me just broke! It felt like I was screaming at the top of my lungs but no one heard. All of this caused me to have issues at home and in school. I was picked on a lot in school. When I would finally fight back, I would black out and when I came to, I realized I had really hurt the person (some even sustained broken bones).

I loved school because it was the one place where I felt safe in every way. When someone threatened that safe haven, I felt like I had to protect it. I wanted to continue to enjoy school, not wanting those feelings from home follow me to my safe haven. As a result, I got suspended a lot. It wasn't because I started the fights, but because of the manner in which I finished them. Everyone knows that telling the teacher on the bully never stops the bully!

I had excellent grades and was always in the gifted and talented programs. I danced, played the flute and the violin as I enjoyed the arts deeply. They were always a therapeutic outlet for me. Raven would take away the only things that brought me any comfort and peace of mind (like music and dance) as a form of punishment but it only developed my expression and appreciation for writing. However it broke me every time.

I had always kept a diary but it was in the sixth grade where I discovered a true passion for writing, thanks to my teacher Mr. M. Poetry became another outlet I would use when music and dance was taken away from me. It was in that same grade where I discovered that I wasn't just a dancer but I could choreograph with such a natural flow. I would just do what I saw in my head. To think I thought my dance teacher hated me because she would scream at me so much but in actuality she saw something in me I couldn't see.

I continued to utilize these artistic expressions to cope with life the best way I knew how but my relief was temporary, nothing seemed to be working!

Every time I was admitted to a mental institution, something inside of me broke even more. I wanted out of that place every time I was put in there. I felt like a caged animal talking to psychiatrists that had no idea what it's like to experience what I had experienced. I would call home to speak to my mother and she would just tell me, "Tell the doctors that you made it all up. Tell them that it was all lies and I'll come and sign you out and bring you home."

Since I wanted out, I did what she asked of me. I wanted to believe that she loved me. Above all else, I longed for that mother/daughter relationship but I eventually realized that I would never get that type of relationship. She never came to sign me out of the hospital. You would think after that happened the first time that I wouldn't have believed her the second time, but I did. Doing that only harmed me and caused me to look crazy. I didn't realize that Raven's plan was working. In fact, at the time I didn't know she had some sort of plan.

She used the fact that I wanted her to love me and not be angry against me so that I was no longer credible. Then I began to fit the description that she was telling others.

"She's always in trouble; she's constantly running away from home with her boyfriend to have sex. She's fighting at school, always getting suspended every time I turn around. She fights me and my husband. Her anger is out of control and she's smoking and drinking too!"

Although what she said was true, the reasons she gave for those behaviors were fabricated! My teen years were truly troubled. That was a fact; but they were my cry for help!

I hated her for not loving me, for not protecting me and choosing her husband over me! I hated her more than I hated him, the one who actually committed the acts. I often wondered if I was really crazy. How would she handle what I was going through? How would she have responded to all this?

After all of that, I believed that I was officially broken, bitter, lost, enraged and seeking revenge was only the beginning!

CHAPTER 3

My First Encounter with the Adult Entertainment World

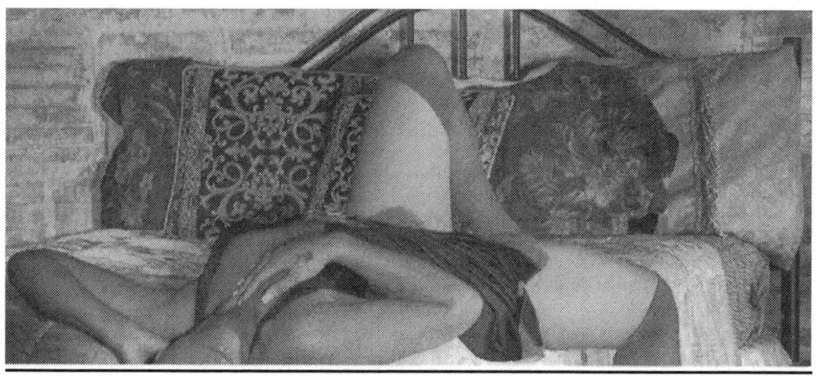

After coming forth to my school, Raven and anyone who would listen about what was happening to me and being hospitalized several times, I was placed in a group home in Long Island. Being there was short lived because it shut down only a few months after. I was then sent to a coed RTC (residential treatment center) in Yonkers, New York. At that time, I had gained quite a bit of weight due to the medication I was taking for depression/*bipolar*. I couldn't understand why my mother never let her husband go but was more than happy to let me go right back into the system.

Maybe it was because he convinced her that I was the problem and that once I was gone, he wouldn't beat on her or the kids anymore and that he would no longer abuse drugs/alcohol since he wouldn't be stressed out? Did he keep his promises?

For a long time, I hated myself. Around this time cigarettes became something I absolutely needed. I had started smoking in the 9th grade to look cool because everyone else did it. It quickly turned into a real vice that helped to release stress. I was so longing for that mother/daughter bond and relationship that my female siblings and I would never get. I knew she blamed me for the investigation and everything else that was going on.

I remember when my little sister told me that they were beat and forced to lie to the social workers. How they made them put their hands on the bible and swear. I began to hate myself even more because I realized that I would no longer be there to protect them. As long as I was there, he wouldn't touch them sexually. If a beating got out of hand then I would literally fight him off my sibling.

Having that over my head was enough of a burden by itself. I enjoyed being overweight because it gave me a break from being desired sexually. I didn't have to worry about sexual things happening to me that I didn't want to happen. That felt great! However, being teased because of my weight didn't feel so great! The other girls at the RTC gave me a ride I will never forget. If you're nice, they take advantage of you. If you're too mean, they feel like they have to prove to you that this is their territory. I didn't say or do much. I was polite to everyone so it was as if I had the word *"Weak"* stamped on my forehead- all because I had manners.

Finally, I got into a fight with the girl that the majority of the campus was afraid of. When I won, I was able to breathe easier because I had earned their *respect.* Group home life was weighing me down and I wanted out. I was so over being depressed and hated not having freedom. So I began weaning myself off my meds and about 3 weeks later, I went AWOL!

I was about 16-years-old around this time. I went home and begged my Mom to let me stay but she called the cops and ambulance instead. So I left. I ran to a nearby park for a while and watched until all the lights were gone. I tried to figure out what I was going to do. I had no I.D., no working papers, no birth certificate and no social security card. I didn't want to go back to the group home! I walked back to my Mom's house and got in the green van that her husband totaled. It was in the back yard of the house.

It was so cold. I tried to keep warm by hugging myself until I finally went numb. The next day, I caught my siblings on their way to school and told them where I was staying. I asked if they could sneak me some food and blankets when they got back.

The next day, I walked around the neighborhood and used the bathroom in nearby stores. This went on for a few days. One day, I ran into an old friend I used to hang with in the neighborhood. We went to elementary school together. Her younger sister and I were in the same class (she was a few years older). I told her what had happen and she offered to let me stay with her at her father's house. She brought me into their basement that her and her sisters shared.

I went back to her dad's place where I got cleaned up and fed. I hung with them for a few days and everything seemed like it was good. Then she dropped the bomb," My dad is starting to notice that the food is going more rapidly than usual. Plus you need clothes and personal things."

I replied, "Damn! What am I going to do?"

She explained what she did to make extra money. "I use this chat line and have the John's pay for the hotel room and my services." I was so grateful to her that I felt indebted to her.

So I sucked it up and agreed to do it! It didn't take much convincing at all. That same night, I probably saw two-three people. That was the night that I made good on my promise. I said when, where and how. Finally I felt like I had some control. Our room was paid up by the first client for 2 nights. Every day we got on chat lines and worked them as best as we could. We were doing well making some money.

At least I was able to take care of myself to some extent. Then it happened! My friend caught her monthly flow (menstrual) and was unable to work. I told her not to worry about it after all she had done for me. I agreed to work for the both of us. So she worked the chat lines and I worked double (I took her Clients and mine). I don't know when she changed exactly, but she started to act like a pimp and she didn't want to work! I had to get out of that situation.

It just so happened that two of my adoptive father's friends were in that same hotel with two other females. It was clear what was going on so I believed that since they knew me, they wouldn't treat me like most pimps treat their girls. Therefore, I decided to go with them. Boy was I wrong! They knew nothing about chat lines and did things the old fashioned way.

At first, it appeared as if I made the right decision. Everyone was so nice. We all ate and had a great time. They all explained to me how the game worked. They told me all of the rules and the dos and don'ts. He told me that when another pimp spoke with me, to quickly get on the street and put my head down. I was never to look in their eyes. He taught us how to look out for cops. Then we got dressed up and walked the strip. The first night, I made nothing because I was too afraid to get in the trick's car. It's one thing when the trick is on your turf, but when you on his turf it becomes a bit more terrifying.

The next day, my pimp gave me a talk. He said, "You need a makeover."

We went shopping. I guess it worked because it gave me a little boost of confidence. The alcohol helped too! What really gave me the push was when he put this baby blue wig on me. It made me feel infamous. That night I made him very happy because the return on his investment was greater than he expected.

It was cool for a while. There were no problems but then my menstrual cycle came. I wasn't feeling good at all and he wasn't happy about me not wanting to work. He said he had a trick for that and that I wouldn't bleed. Then I cursed him out and said, "I'm in pain! What part of that don't you understand?"

He had this look in his eye; I had never seen it before. His best friend and girls immediately left the room. He slapped me across my face. Enraged, I instantly fought back. I refused to just take a beating but I only made it worst. He ripped my clothes off, slammed me against the wall, then onto the bed where he tied me and told me to think about what I was doing.

He left me there for over two days. It felt like forever at the time because I didn't know if he was going to come back. I was left there naked, physically hurt and bruised, hungry, thirsty and humiliated because I was forced to urinate, bleed and defecate on myself. The fumes in the room were unbearable. I refused to scream for help because I didn't want anyone to find me like that. When that happened to me, it completely broke my spirit. I felt utterly worthless! Yet again, I felt that I deserved everything I got.

I began to feel like God just didn't like me. I was so angry. I asked God why all of this was happening to me. I didn't think that my life would ever get any better and that I was born to suffer.

When he came back and cut me loose, I ran to the bathroom to clean myself up right away. We traveled to different areas within the state and to Atlantic City to work. I remember when his bottom girl got out of jail. It was like I was no longer important because his star player was back. I got all the horrible tricks. I remember two *dates* in particular: one smelled of urine as if he wasn't properly cared for. He had an ostomy (aka colostomy bag) and was paralyzed from the waist down. The other was an addict and his choice of drug was crack.

The whole room was filled with this horribly unbearable scent – a scent that I can't really describe. I threw up and had to get out of there. I cleaned up, dressed and kept the money. I got out of there and have never looked back.

CHAPTER 4

The Makings of an Adult Entertainer

I didn't realize that during the time I was AWOL I lost a lot of weight. I had slimmed down to my initial size (before taking the meds and gaining weight). I went back to the group home (RTC).Everyone made comments about my weight loss they asked me, "Are you on drugs?"

For those who mattered to me, I explained how I wasn't on meds anymore and how all that lifestyle was what forced me drop the weight. I didn't even realize that I had lost so much until I got back to the home.

I stayed for a while and made the attempt to get some schooling done and just tried to live as best as I could. I had no intention of leaving the group home again after experiencing all of that. I was doing really well so after their evaluation, they felt I was ready to move to a less restricted cottage on the campus. The one I was in was more restricted since I had to be buzzed through all the doors to enter and to leave. I was so excited about moving to the new cottage because we were given a curfew but there were no buzzing doors. We were free to come and go.

While I was at the RTC, we got a weekly allowance (the most you could receive was $10). In addition to that, we received $125 per season to buy clothes and shoes. That is almost impossible to live on, especially if you have big feet like I do! A pair of sneakers for me was $75. That's not even including tops, jeans, panties, bras, and coats. $125 wasn't cutting it. On top of that, they would take us to places like J.C. Penny and Macy's to shop. Both are expensive.

Unlike a lot of other teenagers at the home, I didn't have the support of my family so whatever I got from the government was it. My roommate, Dana's, closet was packed with fly gear. She had beautiful jewelry. Like me, she had no family giving her anything. One day I asked her "How can you afford these things?"

Dana replied, "I dance in a club and sometimes turn tricks. I can get you on if you want. I have a connection that can get you into the club and hook you up with I.D."

I then asked Dana if she was independent or if her connect was more like a pimp. She reassured me it wasn't like that. We would pay our own way and were responsible for ourselves.

Dancing seemed like a piece of cake. I had been dancing since I could walk so I was excited to make money that way. I agreed, saved up some allowance and then we went to her connection's house. T.J. hooked me up with a fake I.D. for only $20 and told me that he could get me in the Silver Man's strip club in the Bronx.

I went to the club the next night and the manager *"interviewed"* me by asking me to bare all, slowly turn around, and then put my pumps on to slowly turn around again and then bend down. I got the position instantly. T.J introduced me to another stripper that he was really cool with. Her name was "Pinky" because everything she wore was pink which made her milk chocolate complexion pop. She taught me all of the basics: the lingo and how the guys there would act. She even gave me dancewear and let me stay with her for a while.

I remember the first night I danced. It was nothing like I had done before, although there were a few similarities as far as movement itself like when dancing to reggae or some West African movements. I was so nervous that my hands were sweaty. I couldn't hold onto the pole and you could hear my stilettos *click clacking* on the stage because I was shaking so badly! After the first song, my nerves eased up a bit. I thought to myself *'this is not like regular dancing at all.'* I made no money on my first night. After my set was over, I went to the dressing room. I was still shaken up!

Pinky said, "Girl that was horrible. I know its nerves but the customers don't know that it's your first night. If you want to make money, I suggest you think sexy and take some shots because you need them."

That was the point in my life when alcohol and I became best friends. I needed to drink in order to perform.

It wasn't my first drink; I mean my cousins and I used to sneak and drink the adult drinks when they had parties. Plus I used to sneak and take a swig of Dan's southern comfort every now and again just to get through life at home.

In fact, there were times when he would allow me to drink; see Dan was anything but faithful to Raven. He always had someone on the side. We would go on trips to Brooklyn. He would bring me because it was an easy way to get out the house. I was his scapegoat. Raven would never think he would conduct himself in the way that he did with her daughter, me.

This particular side chick had a son. Her and Dan would do coke and give us drinks while we went to his room and chilled. We played games and sometimes even explored each other sexually, although I had no attraction to him. We were just bored.

My point is that by this time in my life, alcohol was nothing new for me. When the shift was over and we went home, I noticed Pinky kept looking at me. She asked me, "Do you know who you look like for real?"

My response was, "My sisters say I look exactly like our mom. They say that I could have been her twin."

Pinky replied, "Okay, but that's not what I was talking about. You look like the rapper Eve. It would be wise of you to play on that. If you do, you won't have to work real hard."

I went on to tell her, "Some dude told me that when I was just 13 years old, around the time Eve first came out but I paid no mind to it. I thought it was a ploy to get in my pants!"

That morning, I looked at some pictures of Eve and practiced doing my makeup the way that she does it. Once the makeup was done I saw the resemblance and I decided to change my stage name to "Eve." I quickly realized that in order to perform well, I had to be tipsy. I needed enough alcohol in my system to relax but not so much that I wasn't aware of my surroundings.

I started making money over the next few nights. My confidence grew and with that confidence, I wasn't afraid to try new things. I began to understand everything Pinky taught me. I became a natural at sizing the guys up. I was able to tell (for the most part) what they liked and how they liked it. It became very easy to become any man's fantasy. Through this experience, I began to learn what drives a man crazy and how to successfully get inside of his head.

It became a formula that I had to learn if I wanted to make money. After all, I was selling every man his own personalized fantasy. I quickly made the money to pay Pinky back for every outfit and shoe given to me. I even had enough left over to give her something towards the rent and food.

I caught back up with Dana when she came to the club to work one night.

"Hey Dana. Where you been?"

She replied, "Dealing with some loyal clients."

She began to tell me about them and how they splurged – how some of them weren't even on the sex tip. They just enjoyed her company. She showed me some gifts they had given her and whispered in my ear the amount she made, which was "$1,800."

I was astonished! I didn't even know those things were possible. I told her to tell them about me. Dana then invited me to hit up the strip after the club, so I agreed.

After work at the club, we hit up the store for supplies and worked the strip. In between tricks, we would talk and catch up. I remember Dana saying that we needed to go back to the RTC soon just to show face and everything. That way we could keep our beds.

Then a pimp came out of nowhere, "You hoes renegading out here?"

I told Dana immediately to get off the side walk, walk in the street, put your head down, say nothing and don't look at him! He shouted a lot of other things and finally left.

Dana was shocked, "Oh my goodness! Where did you learn that from? You just saved our lives."

I explained to her about the other situation I was in and began to educate her on the rules that they taught me.

I told her that if we were really going to do that, then we would have to have each other's back. We also needed a meeting place. Dana agreed.

Even though we had no pimp, it always appeared as though we did because we conducted ourselves with the proper *"etiquette."* We made sure we didn't work the same strip more than two days in a row. All of this would help us not get *"gorilla pimped."* We went our separate ways to gather our belongings and money to go back to the RTC. We didn't want anyone to know that we were AWOL together.

I went shopping and then went back with bags and bags of clothes, boots, shoes and jewelry. That was the last time I went AWOL. There was no need. If I wanted to work, I would just work on the weekends.

After that, my biological father (Lee) came back into my life. He would come visit me. We would go on day passes and soon I was able to get weekend passes to his sister's house in the Bronx. My dad took me shopping and even took me to get my first tattoo, but I chickened out and got my tongue pierced instead. He was loving, understanding and so cool.

I remember the first time I asked him for a cigarette. He looked at me with his glasses below his eyes and said "Um baby girl; you smoke?"

I told him, "Daddy, I'm not going to lie to you. I've been smoking and drinking since I was 14-years-old. It was the only relief I could get at the house."

I went on to explain that my adoptive father Dan kept cigarettes and alcohol in the cabinet and that he would give me anything I wanted to try and keep me quiet.

I told my dad how I would go to the store and purchase cigarettes, beer and alcohol for my adoptive-father when I was just 12-years-old. Sometimes I could do so without money. All I had to do was tell the clerk his name. My father Lee just looked at me in shock and passed me the cigarettes.

While I was on campus, a Library Teacher by the name of Ms. E was like the Mother I never had. She loved God, music and Smokey Robinson. She taught me how a young lady should carry herself and love herself through her program *'A Lady Must'*. Ms. E looked out for me whenever she could so I wouldn't go without. She stressed the importance of education and independence.

She knew about what I had gone through and what I did for money sometimes, yet she never judged me because although she wanted better for me, she remembered when she used to run the streets and date major dope dealers in Harlem. While I was listening to every word she said, I really wanted to do right but something in me wanted to continue exploring this new world I had been introduced to.

I continued to keep up with my studies. I was part of the dance squad, sang on the schools choir, wrote and recited my own poetry. I also recited poetry from famous authors and participated in talent shows. I wanted to join the varsity cheerleading squad but I wasn't welcomed because I didn't have that squeaky clean *girl next door* image. After I tried out, the coach told me that I was really good, especially at dancing. However, she told me that I had to wear my hair a certain way and try a little makeup. How could she make that kind of implication? She was supposed to build us up, not tear us down.

I still wasn't satisfied, even though I had kept my cool. Finally, the day came when the need to explore was much stronger than ever before. I didn't waste my time on boys my age. A 17-year-old wouldn't do. At that point, I wanted to see if what I had learned really worked. Did I really uncover how to get into a guy's head, how to rope him along, and how to become what he needed?

Could I really manipulate any man with my femininity?

I would soon find out!

CHAPTER 5

The Proof was in the Pudding, or was it between my Legs

With this strong desire to see if this new world was real, I began to apply all that I had learned from the strip club. I wore more mature clothes that would accentuate my curves, leaving room for the imagination. I put on makeup and really kept myself up, paying attention to every little detail.

I had learned early on that men rely heavily on all five of their senses. It was successful in the night club and I would soon find out that this theory applied to most men. I transformed from this depressed, overweight girl into a mature lady who was ready to express herself.

I set my eyes on a target – the swimming instructor! Now this man was handsome and other women his age working at the campus wanted him. I took notice to the complements that he constantly gave me. I paid attention to his interaction with the women that he worked with and quickly found his likes and dislikes through mere observation. The swimming instructor hated loud women and would rather interact with a lady who challenged his intellect and possessed a feminine sensuality if you will.

I put my theory to practical use, never throwing myself at him. I would intentionally engage in small talk. Slowly that small talk would turn into conversations and in those conversations, I would find out what I needed to know. A slow, steady buildup of seeing me, hearing me, smelling my aroma, a hug here and there, a caress of my hand here and there. I built his interest slowly but surely!

After all this foreplay, I waited to see what would happen. One day after school, I volunteered to help the swim instructor set up the recreational game room for the following day event. When he turned around from putting some games on the shelf, there I was looking straight into his eyes. I reached past him, pressing my body onto his as I put the game on the shelf. I caressed his shoulder as I came back.

He grabbed my hand and kissed me very passionately, leading me to his office. As he turned me around, he whispered softly in my ear "I want you!"

Then he began to satisfy himself.

I realized that this new world was very much real! I didn't know it then but I had took a chunk out of the forbidden apple! There is power in being a woman and even more power in having what I have between my legs! I had the power I needed to finally make a stand. I set out on this mission to destroy men the way that they had destroyed me. I would use the very thing that they desired against them.

What I didn't know at that time was that the spirit of Jezebel had found her way in and fed off of the vengeance that I so desperately sought after. Everything I had learned and did was an expression of this foul spirit. The manipulation, deceit and becoming whatever he needed or wanted. Doesn't this sound familiar?

I tried to finish my last year of High School but I couldn't stay focused. I was drifting in and out of a state of depression. I guess underneath it all, I was hoping it wasn't real. I was unhappy and empty. I had no real interest in this man and I would only go back occasionally to him because we were compatible in a sexual way. Come to find out that one of my friends and cottage roomies was also seeing the swimming instructor. Their secrets were safe with me. I had a lot of practice on how to keep secrets and became real good at acting like nothing ever happened.

After speaking to my older sister Tammy, I had made a switch from the class I was in to the GED class. The plan was to get my GED before signing myself out of the system. However, that didn't work. I wanted to party, make money and could care less about focusing on my studies.

I signed myself out of the system of New York once I turned 18 and went to live with my sister Tammy in Atlanta, Georgia. I was only missing less than a year of credits so my sister took my transcripts and tried to enroll me in the nearest high school. However, the curriculums were so different that they didn't acknowledge a lot of my credits and test scores. They reduced my credits all the way back to the 9th grade.

I wasn't going to go through High School all over again! My sister and I agreed so I began to look for jobs. My older sister Tammy and I didn't grow up together so we didn't know each other well. All I remembered about her at the time was the last time we came to visit for the summer in Georgia, she tried to make us take naps, clean up all the time, and acted more like a mother than a sister, What really put the icing on the cake was when she snitched on me. I was dating a 30-year-old dude from the Bronx that I had met at work in Brooklyn during the work study program I was in at the time in High school.

I told her in an attempt to bond. She didn't realize it, but she made it worst for me when I got home. My stepfather was possessive about what he felt belonged to him. He didn't want anyone touching his goods! His jealously was sick and very much obvious.

In fact, he always made it hard for me to have a boyfriend at all. It didn't even matter whether they were my age or not. Once, my stepfather made me break up with Peter. We were friends for a long time before we dated. It had only been official for 24 hours.

I had given Peter an innocent kiss on the lips. My stepfather saw and told me to either break up with him or my life was going to be very difficult. I went to Peter with tears in my eyes and told him. Peter hugged me and said, "It's okay."

My stepfather starting yelling, "Hey don't touch her man. Let her go!"

From that point forward, Peter kept his distance.

Tammy and I were not getting along. We just couldn't see eye-to-eye. I spoke with my oldest sister Sasha and she helped me get a job with the company she worked with. Working everyday alleviated some of the tension during the week but I needed something to do on the weekends. I ended up meeting this dude at a club on a Friday Night.

He approached me and said, "I saw you dancing from across the way and I think you're really pretty. Could I get you a drink?"

I agreed and then danced with him the whole night. Even when I tried to dance with someone else, he would find me. His friends made fun of him, saying that he was so open over a dance. He asked for my number and I gave it to him.

I did what I didn't want to do; I started to like him and eventually fell in love and got pregnant. I was 19-years-old at the time, working a customer service job at a call center and pursuing my dreams to make it as a choreographer in the music industry. I did dance auditions every other week. When I wasn't doing auditions, I was choreographing for local upcoming artists or working out.

I didn't find out I was pregnant until one of my sister's best friend got me an audition with a major producer in the industry that had worked with the likes of Ludacris and TLC. He had an upcoming artist that he was working with. I remember his face after I did a freestyle piece to Usher and Omarion. Anyway, the artist had gotten an opportunity to tour as an opening act and the producer told me that I had gained weight and needed to tone down my mid-section.

I assured him it wouldn't be a problem as I knew exactly what to do to get the results I needed. I had to dance! I quickly realized that the method that never failed me appeared not to be working. So I took the test and couldn't believe what my eyes had shown me. That was the last straw for my sister and she kicked me out. So I went to live with my oldest sister Sasha. The baby's father and I were both in agreement that we were not ready for a baby so I decided on an abortion.

Even more so was that I had this huge opportunity to do what I loved and I didn't want to resent my child for taking that away from me. I was very young and immature concerning that matter! I went over to my boyfriend's house after an appointment at the doctors to discuss some things concerning some unwanted results from the tests the Doctor ran. I knocked on the door but there was no answer. I waited a bit no one came. As I walked toward the bus stop, this fool pulled up in his car driving toward the ice cream truck. He was all over some white girl attempting to buy her ice cream.

I lost it completely! I remember blaming him for getting me into that situation to begin with. It seemed as though he moved onto the next.

There was no need to discuss test results because the proof was right in front of my face. I had contracted an STD but was fortunate enough that it was a curable one. It seemed amazing that a client never gave me anything, but my boyfriend did!

I took him back after this horrible episode but it was never the same. I did as I pleased and didn't care how he felt. Later, I went on to have the procedure done. I hated myself for it. I went into a deep depression and I kept having the same nightmare over and over: I was lying on the table in the hospital where I heard and saw a big black garbage bag. Then I heard the sound of something being grounded up and saw parts of the baby's body going into the bag.

I asked God to forgive me but I just couldn't forgive myself. I promised God that if I got myself into that situation again, I would just have to face the consequences and do right by the seed growing inside me. I hated my ex-boyfriend and he reminded me that men are only good for one thing!

CHAPTER 6

Nothing New Under the Sun

I couldn't forgive myself so I forfeited the opportunity at my dream because I resented myself for not having my son. To help take my mind off my pain, I became a busy body. I slept around for a while and when that became boring, I did some amateur nights at the strip clubs. My sister Sasha was very supportive and non-judgmental about me doing amateur nights; plus she loved strip clubs. The same way she drove me to dance auditions and rehearsals was the same way she drove me to the amateur nights at the strip clubs. There was no judgment in her eyes.

I met a stripper by the name of Candy, who put me on to private parties. I would work during the week, do private parties on some weekends and other weekends I would go out to a real party at a regular club.

My sister Sasha told me that she would be moving back to New York in a couple of months so she started helping me find my own place. My sister always stressed the importance of independence, education and not getting pregnant.

She always said "Little girl, I know I don't have to worry about you because you're a survivor. You'll be alright!"

We found a cozy one bed, one bath apartment that I applied for immediately. My sister and her partner at the time helped me furnish the place. Taylor was cool and loving. It was just like having another older sister. I worked, paid my bills and slept around. Sex had no significance to me; it wasn't something I understood. I just did it.

One day, my adoptive mother (Raven) called me, explaining that her church would be in Atlanta for a revival and invited me to come out on that Friday evening. I felt absolutely nothing but I agreed to come anyway. If nothing else, I would get the chance to see my siblings.

So I went to the church on that Friday evening. It was packed. After the service, we all greeted each other and began talking when a woman of God called Prophetess B walked right up to us. She began to introduce herself and explain why she came to us.

She began to speak the word of God, "God wants to bless you. If you just surrender completely and say "yes" by the time you are 21, then you'll be so blessed that everyone around you will be blessed."

She told my mom that the house that she had been looking at in New Jersey was going to come from her daughter (referring to me). She said that her daughter would be able to purchase it if she would just stop fighting God and say "yes."

She went on to say other things and then she dropped the bomb, "God has called you woman of God – a Prophet – you know **his** voice!"

I was 19-years-old and had just received my second prophecy. According to my grandmother, it was my second. My first was when I was just 7-years-old (grandma reminds me of that word spoken every time she gets the chance).

For those of you reading this and are unsure what prophecy is, it's the foretelling of an experience or events to come. A prophet is the messenger of God among other things. I remember not being too sure of what I heard. How is God calling me? My life is a mess!

It began to make sense. All of the dreams and experiences I had as a child. I had realized were different spiritual encounters. So I gave God my "yes."

After that experience, I was determined to try. I went home, got on my knees and repented for everything I had done. I stopped sleeping around and dancing at the strip club. I just worked at a regular job. I began to tithe and go to the church next door to where I lived. One day after work, my chest began to fill heavy and then it felt like a ton of bricks were lying on my chest.

I cried out in fear "God don't take me like this!"

Then I thought that it might be the enemy. Maybe he's mad because I'm trying to do right? I could hear my Grandmother's voice so I started praying and pleading the blood of Jesus. I prayed for my family, close friends, myself and then I began to weep uncontrollably. I started praying for Asia, Africa and the whole world.

I soon realized that what I was feeling on my chest wasn't a heart attack; it wasn't Satan either. It was something supernatural. The more I prayed, the lighter the weight got. When I would pray for certain things, the weight would get heavier. I prayed until I fell asleep.

The next day I told my co-worker (who was also an active Pastor) about the experience and he told me God had burdened me with intercession. For those who don't know, an intercessor is someone who stands in the gap on behalf of a particular person or situation through prayer. He told me that God had allowed me to feel a small fraction of what he feels for whomever or whatever he had me praying for.

Not too long after, I fell into a deep depression. I couldn't stand myself and I was taunted by the voice of the enemy. There was an up roar in the realm of the spirit. It was like I tapped into something and experienced something that the enemy never wanted me to.

He would often taunt me, "Who do you think you are? You'll never be anything close to Godly so why try? What power do you have? God doesn't even notice you. If he did, would your life have been like this?"

I was trying so hard to hold onto the prophetic word given to me. I had even had a few conversations with Prophetess B and she would counsel me. One day I picked up the phone and her number was disconnected. I collapsed, overwhelmed with the fear of my fate. I gave in. I kept saying "Lord I tried," as tears fell from my face!

Feeling lonely, I took a cab to the nearest adult shop. While inside, I came across some adult magazines. I flipped through and realized it was a directory (among other things) for adult entertainment in Atlanta. A few days later, my mom called me talking about my younger sister Tia and asked me if I could take her. She said that she would give $500.00 monthly to help me provide for her. I agreed but thought to myself *'your husband said things would be different once I left. Now you're getting rid of another child!?'*

I wanted to make more money so I thought I should go back to school. I put in my two week notice once everything was set and ready to go for school but they told me to pack my desk that same day. Things were not going according to plan. I didn't want to leave on bad terms so I just did what they asked. I called and told my mom all that had happen and she insisted that it would be okay to take Tia because she would help.

The first month was cool. I went to school and got a job at a pancake house close to where I lived. Plus the funds that Mom promised came through so I enrolled Tia into a Technical college for her G.E.D. and told her not to worry about work. I wanted her to focus on school. Mom was going to help so we would be okay. When the second month came around, I couldn't get my *mother dearest* to answer her phone. Things were getting tight.

After getting an eviction notice, I kicked into survival mode. I had a friend who knew someone that did something with bank accounts and could get up to $1,000. I had done it with no problem but that wasn't enough. So I explained it to my sister and had her do it too. We got some money but it back fired and we wound up owing her bank. I felt bad about it but we needed the money. I promised Tia I would pay it off not to worry!

I met a girl by the name of Ntense at one of the private parties I worked at. She told me about the strip club that she worked at in Atlanta and how she could get me in. I explained to her that I didn't have a permit. I was saving up the money for one. She insisted I come to the club with her anyway, so I did.

During the ride there, she assured me that I would get hired "as soon as management looks at you" she exclaimed. She went on to tell me about this spot next to the club called *'Dirty Tat.'* They hired dancers to dance in the cage. She told me that when the club was slow that she would just go over to Dirty Tat's to make *bread*.

We pulled up to the club and I took in the scenery. It wasn't like the club I did amateur nights at. It was nothing spectacular but it was workable. They hired me on the spot and gave me a few weeks to get my permit.

I worked a few nights every week. When it was slow, Ntense and I would go over to Dirty Tat's. The owner told me the first time we met that he "liked my look." Then he asked if I would be willing to work there part-time, dancing in the cage or doing shower shows. It paid $300 a night plus the tips earned from the patrons. It was just what I needed, so I accepted.

The place was lavish! It was as huge as a warehouse on the inside. There were several private rooms to the right of the entrance and a huge oversized shower built into the wall on the left. Behind that was a big, beautiful lounge area with a fully loaded bar – the largest I had ever seen. There was a second lounge area as well. This place had marble floors with white furniture and touches of gold and silver. It was surreal.

I called one of the adult phone lines from the magazine that I had gotten from the adult shop. They were hiring so I started working as a phone sex operator. While my friends made thousands per week, I was lucky if I made $300. I clearly wasn't any good at it!

I needed some cash fast so I called one of the hiring agencies in that same magazine and told them I was looking to do private parties. The receptionist retrieved some info from me and set up an interview. I explained that I didn't drive so she set it up so that the owner (Ms. Katt) would come to my home.

The next day, I saw Tia off to school and prepared for the interview. There was a knock at the door and I instantly became nervous. I explained my dilemma to Ms. Katt so she gave me an application and some paperwork to fill out. She took some photos of me in my dance wear and then explained to me how it all worked.

I had done two private parties for that agency and it seemed cool. They were professional, very thorough and had a particular process in which they used to screen clients for safety. Everything was great. For a while, I was going to school, working at the pancake house and doing private parties when the work was available.

Then my sister Tia got pregnant and decided to keep the baby. My sister was a healthy girl (a little over weight) so there was no way to physically determine how far she was along. Furthermore, we didn't have any medical coverage or assistance of any kind. I found out about a health department in our county from one of the other dancers I worked with so I decided to take her there.

We were getting ready the next day and I watched my sister walk from the bathroom to the kitchen. Her belly was out and I saw 2 small hand prints. I said to her without any thought, "It's not one baby, it's 2 and they are girls."

We found out that my sister was already five months along. We were worried because she hadn't had any previous prenatal care. They set up an appointment the next day for a prenatal visit so we went to that doctor's appointment and learned that she was having twins and that they were girls.

I'll never forget the look on her face, as my jaw dropped to the floor while the doctor confirmed what I had said earlier. I wondered how I had known that from two hand prints that were visible to me but not to my sister or anyone else. How did I know that? Then I instantly saw myself as a child, a teenager and several instances where I had said and done things like that. The vision quickly dissipated. I never thought much about it after what I had seen.

On that day our lives got real! We had no support because the father decided to go on with his life. We only had four months to prepare for two little ones that might come early because it was a multiple pregnancy. So I contacted one of the dancers I worked with because she also worked in a club. I wanted to see if she could get me in. It wasn't one of the premium clubs in Atlanta, but it was a perfect start. I needed to make the money to get my permit before I could work in those type of clubs. I also had to prepare for my soon to be born nieces.

The money was good but it was unpredictable at times. So I called the agency I worked for and explained my dilemma and she flat out told me that the type of money I was looking for was in escorting. I asked her what was escorting and she explained it to me in detail. It took over two hours for her to explain it. I was overwhelmed with the information I had received but excited about the money I could make.

I took her up on her offer and with the info she gave me, I thought about another stage name and bio. Something realistic yet not true. That's when *Evelyn* was born. I never had to sell myself in this way but I remembered her saying escorts were classy upscale women that men would pay an arm and a leg for. Many women try to call themselves escorts but conduct themselves as prostitutes. An escort's mindset is completely different from a prostitute. They are the forbidden fruit so it's important to create an appeal that seems almost untouchable, but sell the fact that it could be a reality for that lucky refined, affluent gentleman.

I had given her the info she required of me and gave her a few days to advertise. Meanwhile, I was working the clubs and going to school. It was becoming so much that I started falling asleep in class. I stocked up on supplies, sent my sister to her friend's house and created the atmosphere to begin taking clients (playing soft music and lighting candles etc.). Since I had no transportation, I was only able to offer in-calls at the time as an escort.

I was very nervous the first time! I had never done it in that way so it was different for me. I had been exposed to the chat lines, hotels, and street walking, but I had never done it this way. It was so sophisticated and done in excellence. I didn't see dope boys. Instead, I saw affluent men of means. Plus I couldn't get over the fact that with some clients, sex was not involved. I had to sell the fantasy from beginning to end. In the past, it was very straight to the point. This method was done in the same way as a real date.

I instantly became addicted to the money. I could work two days a week and make enough to pay rent five times in a single month. That was after I gave the agency their cut.

Ms. Katt explained to me that I was working in the low end of the industry. She told me that if I invested in myself and really took care of myself, I could charge even more. She went on to explain that I should find a specialty. It needed to be something rare that I do very well, yet something that no one else can do as good as me. The more I could offer, the more I could charge!

I imagined making all of that money and getting us out of debt. I went further into the industry with the intent to provide for myself, my sister and her children that would soon be coming into the world. It was all about the money!

Little did I know that I would soon become completely corrupted. My mind would no longer belong to me and my body was not my own – was it ever my own? I was soon taken over by all the glamour that industry had to offer. Very soon I would be so submerged that I would start to offer her to others!

CHAPTER 7

The Submerging-Waist Deep

Around that time, I had dropped out of school once and re-enrolled. I quit the pancake house and worked full-time as an adult entertainer. I would work at the strip club only on good nights when I felt the need to perform or I felt that I needed to tighten up my body. I basically used the strip club as a gym.

The other nights, I worked as an upscale escort. On average during a slow week, I could pull in approximately $2,000.

Things were beginning to look better! My sister was getting medical attention and the assistance she needed from the government. We were starting to make payments toward the bills. We were even able to start purchasing things for the twins. We had no support so we couldn't have a baby shower. I had to buy everything that they needed.

I finally felt like everything was going to be okay. I completely dropped out of school because working at night and going to school full-time just wasn't meshing well for me. I was able to clear a little over half of our debt by this point. I had also stopped working for Ms. Katt's agency because the cut increased too much.

I tried another agency but there were issues with upper management that caused them to drop the ball professionally so I decided to leave that agency as well.

As a result, I decided to launch out on my own. I felt that I had learned enough to do it myself. That way I wouldn't have to worry about anyone taking a cut. For a time, everything was working out for me. I would see my regular clients who had found me through the agency, but after a while I needed to get new clients. A client called to book me and as the conversation continued, I got this feeling in my gut that urged me not to go. I would then rationalize that feeling with the deadline for this last bank payment and pushed myself to do it anyway.

That was the night I got arrested. I spent two nights in jail. Taylor eventually came to get me out. I had to do probation until the fines were paid off. I knew that was a warning to stop what I was doing but it only took me in deeper. How was I going to provide for us? How would the remaining debt get cleared if I quit? How where the bills going to get paid? How was I going to pay for those fines?

This caused me to research the industry and educate myself more on what I was doing. That's when I realized that the industry was a "world" of its own. I was able to come up with a very sophisticated procedure for screening potential clients to ensure safety and prevent busts.

Tia was still on bed rest and that 1 bedroom wasn't going to adequately house the four of us. Since my lease was coming to an end, I renewed and upgraded to a two bedroom, 2 bath apartment. During that time, I wanted to work less so that I was available to help with my nieces. However, I also needed to maintain the same income if not more.

I remembered Ms. Katt telling me that if I had a specialty then I could charge more. So I decided to really start investing in my *"profession."* I did a professional photo shoot with several looks, got a website designed, invested in the costumes and other tools that I needed. I begin to explore BDSM and set up a page on my site solely dedicated to it.

In doing this, the naked truth presented itself. Femininity wasn't just power but BDSM was power in itself. The money I made for the fetishes and things I entertained was surreal. I enjoyed BDSM; administering those types of services was exhilarating, fascinating and it was fun to see men in that way! I couldn't make since of that world but it excited me in ways that are difficult to describe. One client had booked a session for animal play and the session went like this:

I met him at the door dressed in vinyl black wear from head to toe. I immediately made him remove his clothes and assume the position (i.e. kneel). I gave him the safe word and made him crawl to my playroom (known as a dungeon in BDSM terms). There I instructed him to place the money at my feet. When he did, I quickly collared him and told him that his name was Toby. I walked Toby to the kitchen and fixed Toby some dog food inside of the dog dish. Placed the dog dish on the floor and commanded Toby to eat it all up.

After a while of humiliation, I decided to take Toby on a walk. It was dark outside so I walked Toby around on all fours outside naked. Did you find your spot Toby? Use it! I commanded him. I watched this grown man act like a dog and release bowels like a dog!

After that session, my eyes were opened. I couldn't believe what I had witnessed but I had made $650 just in an hour for this special fetish session.

BDSM made me feel like I was in control of the men who saw me, which was a nice change of pace. I realized that what Ms. Katt had told me was true. The more I could do, the more money I could make.

True to my personality, just doing things was unacceptable. I had to become great at it so whatever I did, I studied it in order to better understand it. This venture led me to a site for sugar babies seeking sugar daddies. I set up a profile and began corresponding. By then, I was really good at quickly finding out what I needed to know.

I went on a couple of actual dates and quickly saw that these affluent men weren't my speed. I was seeking an affluent male a bit more submissive. It was my goal to have at least one *"pay pig"* (bdsm term for a submissive that is financially controlled by the dominant) in my staple of BDSM clientele.

Finally, I found my first submissive sugar daddy. He was a Caucasian man by the name of Brian, a world class business consultant from London. He had been settled in Georgia for some time. He owned a beautiful home in Villa Rica and had two daughters a couple of years older than me. He was into what you would call *sensual domination* and *sissification*. We quickly found that we were compatible.

I decided to conduct a test session to see what Brian's limits were. He gave me a tour of the house and when we stepped into the playroom, my jaw dropped. It was designed like a baby room. The colors were soft pink and white. There was a large oversized crib, changing table and play pen. I couldn't believe my eyes. He explained to me that his last mistress was a live- in mistress and that they were together for about two years. She had introduced him to that type of play without him even realizing it. She had put that room together and after work, he lived his inside life as a baby or female child!

I was completely overwhelmed but tried my best not to show it. Out of all the sessions I had conducted, I had never seen anything like that. There was baby–adult food, baby-adult clothes, girl-adult clothes, wigs and products for body modification. He brought me to a closet and told me that everything in that closet belonged to me. It had been stocked with everything I would need. Amazed at everything I saw, I knew it had to have cost a small fortune to put that room together.

He went on to explain about the custom BDSM shops that specialize in that particular practice. He asked if there was anything else I needed. Stuck in astonishment, I blurted out, "A high chair!" Order a high chair right away with expedited shipping!"

He replied, Right away mistress."

I realized that I needed to familiarize myself with that form of play before conducting a session. I expressed to him going forward that upon my arrival, I was to be served the requested meal, bottle of wine, my favorite chocolates, and the pack of cigarettes. I specified and that my gift (payment) should be presented in an envelope accompanied with an actual gift of gratitude.

We agreed to a monthly allowance of $3,000 plus a shopping spree here and there. I would demand a shopping allowance for fun sometimes just because I could.

Here I was escorting, stripping, and a professional dominatrix who had landed my first submissive sugar daddy or *"pay pig"*. It seemed as though the money had no end. We bought whatever we wanted, never glancing at a price tag. We ate out so much that we forgot what a kitchen looked like. I had jewelry, clothes or whatever guilty pleasure I wanted. It was all within complete reach. I gave money away and helped friends pay their bills. I even helped to bail folks out of jail. I spent money as fast as I made it. On a slow month I was averaging about $7-8,500. When it wasn't slow I averaged about $10-11,000 per month.

Being successful, I became like a magnet. People would come up to me at the strip clubs and say "I heard that you *bank guap* (make a lot of money). Could you put me on?"

Before I knew it, I had my own small agency of upscale women of different ethnicities providing different specialties working for me just by word of mouth. It was never my intention to have my own agency. So I would interview and then train those who I selected out of the bunch. Then those ladies would go on to tell their friends. It all added richly to the other avenues that I made money from.

The club scene was getting boring! I had worked in some of the top strip clubs in Atlanta. I had danced for lots of celebrities and had even been invited back to the homes of a few. I always wanted to travel and to see the world. I had a profile up on one of the sites where adult entertainers found quality work. One day, I checked my inbox and came across an employer seeking to fly exotic dancers from the U.S. to work a duration of up to three months on a contract. They paid for the hotel stay, roundtrip air fare and transportation to and from the club.

Some friends thought I was crazy for entertaining that idea and I completely understood their point, but I was a risk taker and couldn't pass up the opportunity to travel. I had become addicted to the adrenalin that my adventures had offered me. Since I needed more, I began to step up the risk. Luckily it was real. There was nothing crazy going on with the people I decided to work with.

It was just what I needed: more money, a new scene, some sun and a chance to enjoy the beaches. I sent some photos, landed a phone interview and got the job. Since it was my first time, I decided to do a one month contract. I arrived with no problems. I was picked up from the airport and took a boat to where I would be working.

I inhaled deeply as I looked onto the beautiful waters thinking to myself *'this is the life.'* I worked for myself. I got to decide my schedule and make great money. Plus, men were where they belonged – underneath my stilettos!

The men on this island didn't have adult entertainment. This was the only club on the whole island of this kind so it was a complete gold mine. Back at home, the guys at the club want a whole lot of popping, twerking and tricks but on the islands, the men where into truly being entertained. They loved the art of seduction. The performer in me quickly took note and thrived off of that. That is where I transformed from a stripper to an exotic dancer. It was truly about creating the fantasy and sticking to the character while seducing their eyes. I used everything I had learned about roleplay, BDSM and the different types of things guys were secretly into.

Instead of putting on dancewear, I would dress up in a themed costume and be someone different every night. I was always introduced to the stage like this:

Good Evening gentlemen, Welcome this next exotic beauty to the stage: Eve as .....Mistress Illusion (or whoever I was on that night).

Entertaining in that way was a great form of escape from my reality at the time.

During my stay, I sent $300 to $500 to my sister every week so that she could pay bills and take care of herself and the twins. I could easily make over $1-1,500 on certain days of the week there.

When we weren't working, we enjoyed the beaches and the culture. We went shopping and had fine dining. We rarely spent any money because there was always some guy trying to impress or buy us. One gentleman was quite taken with me so he took me to all of the hot spots and introduced me to the best places to eat. That particular evening ended at a beautiful restaurant overlooking the water.

I wanted for nothing. I had money flowing and so many were willing to give me anything within their grasp. After that trip, I was hooked. I began to travel to other places as well. I came back to that first island frequently but as a feature because my act was so rare. It was completely different from **ALL** of the other adult entertainers.

CHAPTER 8

Submerged Completely

At this point in the game, I was very good at what I did. I played the game fairly well and juggled the different aspects of my business. My flow of money was great and the girls that worked with me were satisfied. After developing a good business relationship with the different connections on the different islands (for over a year), I worked out a great monetary deal so that I could send the girls over for monthly contracts.

Everything was so glamorous. I had everything I wanted and needed. My family was taken care of. I began to expand even more by adding more specialties such as Sensual Body Rubs and Role play. That's just to name a couple.

I even had employees on rotation who worked a very well-known swingers club at the time. We provided different types of shows to get the ball rolling. By the time I looked up, I had built an empire with 10 employees in 3 different locations who took nothing but affluent refined clientele. The higher I went, the deeper I got and the more money I made. Through all of this, something kept tugging at me. I would smile, party and have a great time but felt all alone – even when I was in a room full of people.

One night I went to work my shift at the strip club. As usual, I had to get tipsy in order to work. After getting dressed, I went upstairs to the main floor and looked around. The place was packed and money was flowing. I did the usual: made my rounds until it was my turn for the main stage. I went up and did my set. Afterwards, I went back downstairs to shower, change and take a couple more shots. I looked around the dressing room as some girls snorted and popped pills. All of a sudden, I heard, "You don't belong here!"

I went back upstairs to make my rounds for the second time. As I danced for each guy, I would hear different things. At first I thought I was going crazy. Then I realized what was happening. It was the Holy Spirit talking to me. I told the Holy Spirit to "stop messing with my head; I have to work!"

So I kept on working and setting up appointments but I was still unhappy. There were times when I would just get drunk so that I wouldn't feel what I felt. To be honest, I drank pretty often to numb the pain, as I preferred to suffer in silence. I met an intelligent African American guy at the strip club I was working in at the time, His name was Travis and he was completely smitten by me. I felt bad for him because he would come to see me faithfully every week, sometimes twice a week. I knew something had to be up.

One day he asked if he could take me out to lunch and I accepted. We talked and that's when he dropped the bomb on me and said, "I know you are about business and I respect that. However, I want to know you in a more intimate way on consistent bases. Since you are a business woman, I have a business proposal for you."

He went on to make that proposal and I accepted. The proposal was simply that in exchange for some quality time, he would invest in whatever I needed or wanted. He would mentor me   as it pertained to my business. He was the one who taught me how to make everything I was doing legal. We filed the business with the state and began to really make some major moves. As time went on, he held up his end of the deal, as did I. However, he began to grow on me. He was handsome, well groomed, educated and owned everything he had. The thing was he was married. He had the same story that most of my clients had: his wife wasn't paying attention to him. He and his wife were each other's first and they didn't know anyone else. That's why he wanted to *explore.*

Not only was he a great financial support, but he really started to invest in my business once he met the ladies and saw how well it operated. This ride came to an abrupt end when I became pregnant. He made the arrangements to take care it because having a child outside of his marriage wasn't a part of the plan. That was the third time I found myself pregnant and my second abortion – an abortion I had promised God I wouldn't get. I was broken!

After I recouped, I started work again. I knew that something had to change because the twins wouldn't be little for long. So I began to go out and fill out applications for regular Jobs. I got hired at a retail store. It was a seasonal position and after working through one pay period I couldn't do it anymore. I looked at the check in disbelief and thought that I couldn't live off of that. I made many attempts to leave the industry but the money always brought me back.

At that point most of the girls from my agency had decided to leave because of my back and forth between regular jobs. I had decided to get a new website and reinvent the look of my business. All the while I felt trapped; I wanted better but couldn't get better so I was right back where I started. How did I get there again? How did I get so deep to where it seemed I couldn't get out?

Since most of the girls were leaving, I was more focused on getting my weight up. I worked twice as hard and threw myself into work doing photo shoots, private parties, body rub sessions, domination sessions, escort sessions, alternating shifts at the strip clubs and keeping up with my sugar daddy. The money was great but I was completely numb and my heart grew colder with each passing day.

The game changed and work wasn't the same. Then it started to slow up when amateurs hit the scene with a street walker's mentality. They started giving their time for as low as $50. Once clients realized that they could save money, it all started to dry up a bit. The exception was those few clients who looked for quality.

Those were the ones who did what they did for "different" reasons. The clients that were loyal are called "regulars." It was a time when adult entertainers had to rely on their reputation and reviews to help solidify their *quality work* to get hired.

While this was happening, I noticed that the caliber of clientele started to change. Clients felt like they could negotiate. In addition, there was an ongoing crack down so it became extremely risky. I began to slack off on escort sessions.

I split work between private parties and body rub sessions. I was empty and void of myself. I couldn't feel anything; I just followed through with the routine. I just went through the motions.

I came alive when I went out to party. It was like that every time I hit the dance floor. During those moments, I was safe, happy, and satisfied. I was a better version of myself. When the song was over the reality would set in and I would order another drink.

CHAPTER 9

In My Skin or Out of My Skin?

Time went on and I was celebrating my birthday with one of the girls (Mocha) who worked with me. This consisted of working hard to get our weight up and splurging like we had lost our minds. Our motto was to *"Party like a rock star."*

At that point, we had been celebrating the whole month of February and well into March. Mocha decided to take me out to a place nearby that was known for ladies night. I met her at her crib (house) and there were two guys with her. I guess she was hooking me up with a date. I wasn't too happy about it, she knew where I stood as it pertained to relationships.

We arrived at the club. It was live and I was ready to hit the dance floor. I felt bad for the guys because as soon as they bought our first drink, I went straight to the dance floor. I wore a red corset trimmed in black, black leather leggings, black pumps that could kill and flawless makeup with a bold red lip that would take your breath away. I danced with my girl Mocha. We did dance a little with the guys who brought us to the club but I ended up by myself, like I always did – getting lost in the music and the movement.

I took a break and went to the bar and a group of women were staring at me. I had never gotten so much attention from a group of women like that. At first, I thought they were sizing me up until one of them broke the silence, "I see you out there on the dance floor. Your dancing is amazing and you're beautiful."

They all started telling me how pretty I was so I replied with a polite "thank you." One of those women finally introduced herself, "Hi. My name is Yoli and I have a friend I would like you to meet."

I replied with one simple word, "Okay."

I was buzzing from the alcohol and having a great time. Their friend must have been a really shy guy if he needed them to help him. Once we got to the other side of the club, I realized her friend wasn't a ***he,*** but a ***she***! She introduced us to each other and left.

We made small talk for a bit until she asked me if I wanted to dance. After dancing, she asked me what I was drinking and then ordered me a drink.

Afterwards, I went back to hang out with my friend. When the night was over, Tae came back over to where I was and told me, "I'm only here for a few more days and I would like to chill with you while I'm here." I ended up giving her my number before leaving.

The next day, I got a phone call from her and we arranged for her to come by that same day. We enjoyed each other's company so much that we spent the next few days together. We talked about things that I had never shared with anyone else. I had never experienced that with anyone. It was like we were deeply connected on so many levels. I couldn't believe how much we connected, even spiritually. The second day we spent together I told Tae about a dream that I had when I was just 13 yrs old. I went on to say……

The dream felt so real that I literally woke up drenched in sweat. On that night, Dan never came to the basement. I dreamed that I was at this camp (this camp looked similar to the one we use to go to in the summer as kids) and people were sitting around the fire. Then I began to worship. As I worshipped, I danced around the fire. Afterwards we all got ready to go to our cabins for bed. As soon as I laid on my bunk, I fell fast asleep.

I was in this place and there were many, many people in line. You could hear the music around the corner. As the line moved, I could tell I was getting closer to the entrance. I could feel the excitement radiate from everyone; it was like this place was the hottest thing around. As I got closer, I noticed a man in a trench coat with the collar up and a hat cocked toward his face. So I was unable to see his face.

As I was moving more toward the middle of the line, Jesus came to me and placed a watch on my wrist. He told me to press the button on the side of the watch when I needed him. When I got inside, I realized it was a huge club of some sort. I went to the bar and watched.

There were strobe lights everywhere with people dancing all over. It seemed as though there were thousands of people crammed into that club. As the people danced, I noticed they looked wet. My eyes open and all of a sudden there was this moment of clarity. I realized the people weren't dancing but they were scratching themselves and grabbing at their clothes. They weren't singing; they were screaming in torment. They weren't wet from sweat but from the heat. All of a sudden, I was burning up and I realized that I was in hell. I pressed the button on the side of the watch and woke up in heaven. I was sitting in a chair with a typewriter in front of me.

The Lord was walking back and forth. He told me, "Everything I tell you, you must record it!"

There was such a feeling of crucial intent behind his voice. It seemed as though I was writing something of grave importance. I asked God about my mom and sister who had passed away when I was younger. They were fine. All of sudden, the enemy appeared. It was the same man in the trench coat and hat from before. Suddenly they were in a boxing ring and I was sitting in the front row. They were fighting! Jesus had taken somewhat of a beating; he was bruised and bloody. It wasn't looking too good. Then the tables turned and Jesus knocked out the enemy. I abruptly woke up drenched in sweat.

I remember going upstairs to my Mom's room crying and asking to speak to my grandmother. I felt like she would be the only one who could understand. My grandmother tried to console me but could barely understand a word I said. So she just prayed for me over the phone. I couldn't make since of the dream. I was frightened by everything that I saw in the dream. I would go on to later receive a full revelation and interpretation of this dream.

Afterwards Tae said there were two things that were very clear and they were that I had a call on my life and that I was prophetic. She also stated that it was clear that the enemy was trying to stop me from fulfilling the call on my life.

However we also discovered that we were both *"over it"* as it pertained to God and church. Tae was running because she was excommunicated from her previous fellowship and it made her feel as though God didn't want anything to do with her.

I was running from God because I didn't want anything to do with church and so called Christians; they were the ones that harmed, hurt and abused me the most. I felt as though God had abandoned me. So here we were; two people over it – or so we thought!

After spending a few days together and getting to know each other a little bit, Tae left to go back home. Tae lived in another state. We both realized that we wanted to continue to get to know one another so she arranged for me to come to her hometown. Before I could pack, there was something I felt she had to know so I called her.

“There is something I have to tell you.”

Tae replied “What!?”

I began by saying, “Remember when I told you that I dance? Well I do more than just dance.”

I wouldn’t say it straight out because I was scared of what she might think or even do, but it was her right to know. I had her guess until she guessed right.

Her response was, “I don’t care; sometimes people have to do what they have to do.”

I packed with excitement and visited with her for two weeks. I had an amazing time. She treated me like a queen; she treated me with so much respect. It was like a red carpet was laid out just for me. When I got back home, reality hit me and I went back to work. Tae called me saying that she fell in love with me during our visit and that she wanted to be with me. However, she couldn’t be with someone who wasn’t hers only so she asked if I was willing to stop dancing and escorting.

I told her that I was more than willing and that I could do sensual body rubs. I went on to explain what that was and what it all consisted of. I even convinced her to let me keep one domination client which was more like a sugar daddy or *"pay pig"* if you will. She wasn't thrilled about it but she understood that a transitional period would be necessary. Plus it was way better than all the other stuff I was doing or so I thought.

She came down to visit for a month about two to three weeks after my visit with her. During the visit, she decided to move to Atlanta so she could be close to me. She went back to Texas to get everything situated and to prepare for the move. Once she came back permanently, I was very excited and even felt as though this relationship would be the greatest thing for me. We began to look at new places together as my lease was almost up and it was only right to have a place that was mutually ours.

When we finally moved to our new place, I was so happy that I didn't work at all. I looked for a job but soon I became depressed because I was accustomed to a particular life style. Not being able to buy what I wanted when I wanted depressed me. Tae took care of everything financially. All of the bills were paid and our needs were met but having an empty shoe box and an empty safe truly got to me.

I told Tae that I needed to start working with body rubs like we agreed on. She tried to convince me there was no need but I insisted. Slowly but surely, I started to look at all the sites that I knew about online to see if the money was still flowing in that area. I posted an ad to see what it would do. I set up the sun room area of the apartment as my work station. I invested in everything I needed for body rubs so that I could get started.

True to my nature, I aim to be the best at everything I do so I read several books on the art of massage. With the knowledge I gained, I was able to come up with great services and add-ons that would make me more marketable. I offered packages that were the ultimate pampering so that when a client experienced it, they would feel as though they were receiving a spa-like experience.

At first, I didn't get many calls. I would go on to learn that that was one of the consequences for leaving the industry, even if it's only temporary. I couldn't point out the fact that I had reviews because they were for services that I no longer offered. It was important to not send the wrong message.

I had to reinvent my look and my bio as a sensual body rub artist in a way that was marketable. With a new look and new website, I was ready to try again. The second time worked like a charm!

I knew that reviews were extremely important because they solidified your work and reputation. Therefore, I offered a small discount to those who were members of a review site to get reviews up quickly as a sensual body rub artist. This helped out a lot and I began to experience a steady flow of calls. It was nothing impressive, just steady. At that point, I still wasn't satisfied because a service like that did not make a whole lot of money.

Saturation didn't bother me because the industry always has a lot of girls. It was the pricing that bothered me. The average rate for a sensual body rub for 30 minutes was $50 while the average for an hour was $80. My average daily for sensual body rubs was $300, which for me seemed like a major setback. Once I was able to provide add on services, a bad day was about $600-800. If others were working, then it was between $1,000 to $2,000. . That meant I would have to work harder but I preferred to work smarter.

So I called my girl Mocha, who used to work for my agency, to let her know what I was trying to do and she was up for it. So everything I had to do for myself, I did for her. I trained her on how our services were executed, as well as the whole reinvention process.

We added doubles to the list of services to help drive more income and it seemed to be working. I learned quickly when the *'hot zones'* in this market were. *Hot zones* are days and time frames when business is more lucrative. I based our availability on that as well and began to see a bit of a difference.

So we worked and started developing regular clientele. This one guy by the name of Craig booked a session for an hour and quickly became a fan. He booked appointments twice per month; sometimes he even booked one session every week. He had officially added us to his budget and his goal was to try every service we offered. Things were going well with business and I felt better now that I was making money, even though the money flow wasn't the same.

During the winter season after Christmas just before Thanksgiving; Craig booked an Erotic Extravaganza which was a fancy way of saying sensual body rub party. We corresponded accordingly to set everything up just right. Mocha wasn't available so I had to find two other girls to do this party with. I called up Santia and Mia to see if they were available to do it. Those were two young ladies who had worked for my agency in the past. They were up for it so we met up. I gave them a quick briefing on how services were executed. I told them this was a regular client and to please put their best foot forward.

The night of the party, I packed my work bag with everything I needed to do the job. As I was packing, Tae came in the room and asked why I was packing dance shoes and a striper outfit. I got extremely angry and we argued.

"I thought you weren't dancing anymore. Is this really a private party?"

I explained that it wasn't even like that but I could tell that she didn't believe a word I said. So we argued some more. I left extremely pissed off! When the girls and I arrived at Craig's house, there were three other guys there as well. They had a seafood broil going, drinks were flowing and they were all playing poker.

Craig introduced everyone and I asked for a drink. I needed to shift my focus. It was time to get that money! Everyone mixed, mingled and the dudes were choosing. One guy left but the night continued on with music, drinks and conversation. Craig and I went to his room and I set up the massage table and got everything ready. We had already agreed to an add-on to his service when we were corresponding initially. Up until that point, I was doing okay but I wanted the money.

So when the time was just right, I gave him that experience! Once the girls and I made our money, they gave me my referral fee. We got ourselves together and left. When I got home, I was expecting

Tae to be sleeping but she wasn't. She started drilling me with questions so I finally asked her, "Why are you interrogating me?".

When I found out that she went through my emails, I was livid! She knew what I had done by reading my emails that were exchanged between Craig and I. She had also found the escort website that I had been working on that week. We had a huge blow out and I broke up with her. I told her that I wanted her gone!

She then told me that if I really wanted her gone then I should book her flight for her so she could go back home. I booked her flight and then left for my sister's house.

I had a thousand mixed emotions going on but one thing I was clear on was that I needed to make money so I could get my own place. I had officially returned completely to the industry. When I arrived at my sister's house, I explained what happened and how I needed a temporary place to stay until I got the money. I assured her that it wouldn't be long at all.

The next day, my sister's husband told me about a friend who rented out his spot to people who were in that line of work. I asked him to hook it up and met with that guy later on that day. I took a look at his place and we negotiated a price. I began working the next day. There was a huge influx of calls. I was truly missed by my regulars.

Those regulars came to see me and booked overnight sessions. The money was great and I felt like I really was back. In the meantime, Tae kept calling me. She asked if she could just talk to me face-to-face but I didn't think that was a good idea. I apologized for hurting her but was sure that the break up was best for both of us.

After one week of working, I had enough money to get my own apartment and fully furnish it. I even had money to spare. However, I didn't get one. I had a bunch of associates who owned their own businesses so it was nothing to get checks and or check stubs to prove my income. Plus I had good renter's history.

I stayed at my sister's and kept working at the spot. I finally let Tae come see me. I figured that she had to be the reason why I didn't just go and get my own place. Maybe I did need closure?

She came by that night and we talked. I apologized again. We didn't have time to finish the conversation so Tae asked if she could come by again to finish it. I told her that I would let her know of a good time.

I continued working for the next couple of days but it seemed like my attitude had changed. I wasn't as concerned about getting a bunch of money. It was like I was slowing down or something. I asked Mocha if she wanted to do body rubs during the day and she was up for it.

Tae came over twice. The last time she came by, she asked me why I couldn't just stop. She wanted me to promise her it would never happen again but I couldn't make that promise. In fact, I told her that I would not make any promises of stopping and I didn't know if I even could.

There was so much going on in my head that was destroying me little-by-little. The feeling of being in my skin, yet out of my skin at the same time was overwhelming! I told her that I wasn't sure about this whole being with a woman thing either. I felt conflicted; on one hand I loved and cared for her but on the other, being in the relationship was draining for me. I told her how unsure I was about these things.

She told me, "I'm not giving up on you!

I couldn't understand why she wouldn't just walk away. What was it that made her want to stay after all the crap we had experienced and all that I put her through? I felt as though I wasn't good enough for her. All of her friends told her to just leave me anyway. There were even times when she wanted to leave but she never did.

I didn't realize it right away but soon enough I saw that no matter what craziness I did to try to push her away she stayed. I realized that I really didn't know what love was or what it looked like until Tae came into my life. My mind was so far gone that I wasn't able to see the value she added to my life. I realized I had hurt this beautiful pure gift I had been given over and over again. I had hurt the very one and only one who ever truly loved me genuinely wanting nothing from me. She didn't deserve this and she certainly didn't deserve to pay for what others had done to me in my past.

Eventually I decided to go back home and try my best to do body rubs only! I hired three other exotic sensual masseuses in hopes that it would limit my physical participation and increase my income at the same time.

At that time, our lease was up and we decided to move instead of renewing. We moved to a new luxury three bedroom, two bath apartment. I set up the second room as my work room and stocked it with everything that was needed to do the work. I set up the third room for those that booked our packaged services because the bathroom was conveniently right there. The third room was also used by another sensual body rub artist when 2 girls were scheduled to work the same time.

I advertised for the other girls, screened and booked their appointments according to their scheduled availability to work. I trained them on the proper protocols for everything, showed them where everything was located and educated them how to sell our packages and services. I then went on to teach them about the type of clients we want to attract. They had to learn what great customer service was and looked like from us to the client.

I scheduled one of my regulars for each young lady to do a double with me. That way they can see firsthand how to best service clients. This session was their final test – it either ended their training or prolonged their training. We worked a lot, doing private events and parties. The money was getting real good.

It was calm for a while. I never admitted this to Tae, but there was something that I started to realize. I had a disease and its name was *"adult entertainment."* It had taken over my mind, distorted my perspective and sight. I became its slave willing to serve it blindly, not realizing all the damage that was taking place mentally, emotionally and spiritually. The world of adult entertainment became a disease and there seemed to be no cure. In order to get out, I had to recognize the hold that it truly had on me and that I couldn't do it on my own. It was more like a functional addiction. It felt like I had everything under control but it was really controlling me.

No matter how much I drank or smoked, there was nothing that would be able to help me cope with what I was doing to myself. Would I ever be able to kick this habit?

On another note, I came to realize that I had fallen in love with someone who saw me for who I truly was. Someone who saw past what I was doing and saw the potential that was lying dormant inside of me. Someone who saw what God saw in me- the reason I was put here on this earth, she saw my purpose.

I fell in love with someone who protects me, covers me and prays for me when I didn't and don't have the strength to pray for myself. I fell in love with someone who yielded to and partnered with God to help usher in my deliverance, even when it was a painful position to be in. I don't know anyone that would be willing or have the endurance to go through all that we had to go through just to get to where we are today. I know that God gifted Tae with a special love just for me!

CHAPTER 10

Freedom!

Jessie, a friend that I went to school with, came over to the house one day. During her visit, she began to tell us about this church that she was visiting. She expressed how powerful the word was and how awesome the worship experience was. I told her that I didn't think it would be a good idea because I didn't want Tae and I to be attacked. She expressed how this church was open to ALL people, no matter who you were!

Although it sounded awesome, I was reluctant to attend but Tae really wanted to see what this ministry was about. So we decided to visit that week. I couldn't really experience the service because my heart was still hardened. I didn't really want to hear much of anything due to past experiences. Tae was more receptive and open to the service. It was more like she had been waiting for that opportunity to find out if there was more to it than she had been taught.

Tae eventually joined the church and rededicated her life to Christ. It became difficult for us because she was getting her life together and I still wanted to do what I wanted to do. I wasn't very nice or accommodating to her. I would make comments of her being, "Holier than thou." I would tell her to "go and be with your little church friends." In return she continued to pray for me.

I would visit the church every now and then but my main focus was still on making money. At that time, I was limited on how I made it because I was committed to our relationship. However, the desire to maintain the lifestyle or mentality I had acquired by making fast money had already taken over. At times, I felt like there wasn't room for anything else.

I don't remember exactly which month it was but I do know it was toward the end of the summer when I finally joined the church. I remember that day like it was yesterday. I had on a mustard yellow summer dress with an oversized black flower on the front of it. I wore my favorite blue cropped jean jacket that had hints of yellow in it with jet black sandals echoing my jet black hair which was cut in a faux Mohawk style.

During the service, I started to experience what felt like a melting or warming in my chest. I began to see myself and the state I was in. When the Preacher asked if there was anyone else that wanted to join the church and give their life to Christ, I said *yes* on the inside. I tried to move my feet to come up to the front but my legs were frozen. It felt like my legs instantly turned to sand; they felt like the heaviest sand bags ever!

I struggled to move even more when the Preacher asked if there was anyone else. It was like I broke free. I got up and walked to the front. On that summer day, I joined the church and rededicated my life to Christ!

This was where my road to redemption truly began! I had grown up in church, initially receiving salvation at the age of seven and because of that; I assumed it would be easy. That's when I realized that I knew of Jesus Christ but I didn't know him for myself. There was a huge difference in having knowledge about someone and having a relationship with that person. The one thing that was very clear to me was that my job in adult entertainment had to go, but that wouldn't be an easy thing to do!

It was a battle that I wasn't prepared for but a battle I was willing to fight. Things were going well. I continued to go to church but I also continued to do sensual body rubs to maintain income. At that time, I only smoked when I was angry or drinking alcohol, which was still too frequent. I didn't drink as much when Tae and I got together, but it was still a bad habit that I needed to conquer.

One fateful February day, Tae and I were watching the story of Abraham. I was spiritually moved by that movie. His faith astonished me! He had the ability to obey the voice of God! I told Tae, "I feel as though I should fast for five days, eating only fruit, nuts and yogurt."

I went on to tell her, "I never fasted growing up but the adults in the church would fast. It was a time that they would become closer to God!"

That need to fast just came out of nowhere. I felt strongly that it was an urge that only heaven could give, so I fasted for five days. The fast ended on my birthday, February 19th.

During my fast, I repented a lot, cried a lot and prayed a lot. I spent most of my time with the Lord, reading the bible, watching bible stories and listening to contemporary gospel music. Everything seemed as though it was the same. I didn't feel anything different on day one of the fast but I continued anyway because I truly believed that I was supposed to be on that fast. I didn't give up!

During the remainder of the fast, I experienced the most incredible times of worship. At times I just knew God had to be somewhere near because I could feel a presence in the room. It felt like someone was right there with me but I just couldn't see him.

I felt refreshed and rejuvenated once the fast was over. I had a wonderful birthday. I spent my day with Tae and two other good friends; Kirk and Allan. That night we got ready for my birthday party that Tae put together.

I had an awesome time with everyone. My cake and cupcakes were hello kitty-themed. The food, music and drinks were perfect. My friends were sure to keep the drinks flowing. I didn't really realize how much good the fast really did me until my birthday party. I really didn't have too much of an appetite but I had to eat so that drinking wouldn't make me sick.

I got sick anyway. As Tae held my hair back, I began to slur, "I'm sorry God. Why can't I drink anymore? What did you do to me?"

I realized that my capacity to consume alcohol had changed, among so many other things. For starters, my taste for alcohol and cigarettes were gone. God had literally taken the taste and appetite away. Looking back, I can't believe how excessive it was for me.

Another thing was that the people who were at my table at the party were a mixture. There were those who I worked with in the adult entertainment industry. There were also people from church, as well as close family and friends. This was symbolic to where I was at that time in my life. I had one foot in sanctification and the other still in adult entertainment.

I had never felt like that before. I felt clean on the inside but still wasn't quite where I needed to be. I was becoming a different person on the inside but it felt like a container that had taken in something that didn't belong! There was a newness taking place that the fast had ushered in but I didn't realize it until I was drunk. Talk about things that will make you laugh!

Time went on and I continued to go to church while still working. I was enjoying this awesome newness. I looked forward to the complete change. We were doing sensual massages only until one day I slipped up. A client booked an appointment. I went about everything in the usual way and followed the proper protocols. I prepared everything as usual but little did I know that it wouldn't be a usual appointment.

I answered the door and there stood this tall, dark and handsome man – well-groomed and fit. I greeted him, asked to see ID and asked if he would like anything to drink. He told me no so I showed him to the room and began to play the therapeutic music. Then I left to give him a few minutes to prepare.

I warmed the oils and came back ready to begin the session. Everything was going smoothly and then he touched me with a rubbing motion on the sides of my thighs and immediately my womanhood kicked into overdrive. It was so weird. I didn't know this man but his touch seemed so familiar. It was like we had chemistry, a silent tension that I ignored! He had booked an hour but decided to extend his session 30 more minutes.

After he left, Tae was extremely mad.

"Why didn't you text me back? I thought it was only for an hour!

We got into a bad fight and broke up again!

I felt suffocated because she was constantly drilling me with questions about clients all of the time. However, I also felt guilty because I didn't stop him from touching me. It was like something inside of me connected to his touch. I knew she had a reason for her feelings because of my track record but I just couldn't handle that. I was also drained by all the constant influx of emotions; I didn't know how to handle that either.

The gentleman became a regular. It seemed as if his goal was to wear me down but I felt that I was strong enough to withstand that temptation – or was I? We talked during his sessions and I learned about him quickly.

I learned how his wife to be and the mother of his children died of cancer, leaving him as a single parent of two. It melted my heart and I thought to myself that *they don't make them like this any-more*. I was confused because there was an important rule in my business. That rule was to never get personal with a client. Keep it professional at all times. I was curious about this guy but I completely forgot that curiosity kills the cat in the end!

At the end of one session, he dropped the bomb on me.

"I know that this may seem awkward but I can't help but feel more about you. Would you afford me the opportunity to take you out to dinner? I just want to get to know you more. I have no problem paying for that time."

Then he placed five crisp hundred-dollar bills in my hand and told me, "Think about it."

He later sent me a text message as a reminder that stated the same thing. He seemed like the perfect gentlemen. I didn't realize that I was being pulled in a backward direction at the time. If this was a test, I would soon fail with a big fat F because I gave in and allowed him to take me on a date. I got ready and was actually excited to see what it was all about.

He picked me up from the house and took me to the cutest little place. We ate and talked. When I tried to decide which dessert to order, he ordered all of them for me to try!

I was so flattered by his gesture that I blushed. He fed me a sample of every last one while asking my opinion of each dessert. Afterwards, we retired to a nearby hotel for some R&R. One thing led to another and before I knew it, I was completely swept away in a whirlwind of physical pleasure.

It was like we were both insatiably filled with extreme desire for one another. Once we finally came down from our high and got off of the pleasure zone ride, he told me that he had received a job offer back in New York. He wanted me to go back with him. He couldn't have been serious!

He told me that he was dead serious. His exact words were:

"Find out how much it would cost to break your lease and I'll give it to you. Sell or throw away whatever you don't need. Start over with me and I'll take care of you."

I took in a huge gulp of air, I mean I've heard men say and offer all types of things but for me this topped it all. I had been offered cars, houses, condos and I even had one guy profess his undying love to me on one knee with a ring. I couldn't believe what I heard. I knew what those other men were about and why they offered the things that they offered to me but this felt so different. He just told me to think about it and that he would be leaving at the end of the month.

I was floating on air with butterflies in my tummy but as the key turned and I opened the door, reality hit me harder than a train. Tae was sleeping on the couch. I tried not to wake her but when I looked up, her eyes met mine and they began to well up with tears. She was so emotional, “I know that you’ve been out with someone! We just broke up!”

We went our separate ways within the house. This went on for about a week and Tae started talking with her ex. We wound up having an argument and decided that we really needed to make changes immediately. In the middle of arguing, Tae got on the computer and looked for a flight. She had gotten it altogether and said, “If you really want me to leave click the pay button.”

I walked right up to the computer and clicked it.

That Sunday we both went to church. The Preacher did an altar call for couples. I grabbed Tae’s hand and we went up to the area to receive prayer. It was clear that I had decided to work on the relationship instead of leaving. When we got home, we talked about everything and decided to let each party know that we had decided to work on our relationship. We did that by placing those phone calls.

At Church, there was an announcement for those interested in joining the dance ministry. Of course, I knew that announcement was for me. I was seven-years-old the first time I saw liturgical dance and it was at a church in Brooklyn. I watched in awe as the lady danced by herself, wearing a red long sleeve garment. I wanted to be like her when I grew up. She danced with boldness, conviction, power and unapologetically.

My grandma took me to meet her after the service and that's when the apostle of that church spoke prophetically over me – the word that grandma never lets me forget. When I heard the announcement, I knew that it was what I was supposed to be doing! I joined the dance ministry about six or seven months after joining the church and rededicating my life to Christ.

It was one of the best decisions I have ever made. I was still doing body rubs at the time but it had become less of a desire. I invested my time in rehearsals and fellowship with the dance ministry instead of making money. It got to the point where I said, "I cannot be before God and people while still acting like this."

I couldn't be in adult entertainment while also being a part of the church. I knew that changes had to be made! I finally understood exactly what it meant to "offer yourself as a living sacrifice" according to Romans 12:1. My journey in pursuit of purity gave me freedom.

I began to experience freedom from various things! I had already been freed from being an alcoholic. I had been freed from smoking cigarettes. For a while, I would cave in when I was angry or under massive stress and have a drink and a cigarette. There were even a couple of times where I drank or smoked just to fit in. Every time I did, I would feel sick afterwards so I quickly learned not to pick back up what God freed me from.

The first time the dance ministry ministered together it was to a song called *'Joy.'* I will try to describe how I felt:

It was as though it was just the Lord and I dancing. I gave him everything that I had through my movement. There were silent cries that no one heard but the Lord. It was like I was speaking without saying a word.

Once the service was over, the Prophets of the House came to me. Mother D told me:

"Continue to consecrate yourself to God. Woman of God continue to seek purity! There is a strong anointing that God has placed on your life. In two years, God will use the dance ministry to break strongholds and bring you before great men and women of God. If not as a whole, then God will use you!"

I broke down crying and fell to my knees. No one knew what my struggles were – how my heart desired to be pleasing in the sight of God. They didn't know what I had been trying to accomplish spiritually. I knew God was speaking through her directly to me!

When I got home, I laid on my couch by the wall towards the main door. I felt so tired, drained and empty. I had never felt anything like that before.

I fell asleep on the couch and woke up screaming "I'm on fire!"

Tae and my sister came rushing out of their rooms, asking me if I was okay but all I could do was scream, shake and kick. I was burning up from my abdominal area down to my feet. I kept rubbing myself everywhere to put out this fire that I couldn't see.

They finally calmed me down but by then, I had no voice. I'm sure they thought I was crazy. After a little while, I drifted back to sleep. I had no energy; I felt so drained that I couldn't eat. I could barely make it to the bathroom.

This went on for three days. I didn't know it then, but there was a purge that took place during those three days. In my ongoing pursuit, I wanted to be filled by the Spirit of God. After a while, I received the the Holy Spirit with the evidence of speaking in tongues. This was one of the happiest days of my life. I felt as though I was getting closer to God.

A lady by the name of Camara was an associate Pastor at my church. She was the first to recognize the prophetic calling on my life. We spoke about my life on a personal level. We developed a relationship in which she mentored and counseled me. She held me accountable and gave me a lot of materials to study.

Camara helped me to become aware of whom I really was. She taught me about spiritual disciplines and the need we have for them as a believer and one who is called to the office of a Prophet. She helped me work through some of my mess while never judging me. Instead, she loved me.

One day we were at her home and she asked me if I really wanted to be filled with the Holy Spirit. I jumped at the opportunity! After she talked about what happened in the book of Acts on the day of Pentecost, she asked me again if I wanted to be filled and if I believed that the Holy Spirit would come. After I answered "yes," all I remember was feeling something come over me in such a way I could no longer feel my body.

I wasn't sure if I was even breathing. I began to weep and my body continued to go numb. It felt as though my body was swelling up. I began to speak in an unknown language but it wasn't fluent so I began to doubt. However, I knew that was the day that the Holy Spirit filled me. That Sunday, it just so happened that the Pastor did a call for those who wanted to be filled with the Holy Ghost. I went to the altar and Pastor Camara laid hands on me, as did two other elders. I spoke fluently. The entire experience is unforgettable.

I was extremely excited about this ongoing change and continued to make progress. I looked up educational programs so that I could find a trade and enter work quicker. I tried cosmetology school but they told me the high school diploma I had wasn't real. I asked them what they meant so they explained that the $300 online program I took was a scam. Testing like that had to be done in person at an approved school or facility.

I felt knocked down, again! I called the online program to try and get my money back but they gave me the run around and never returned any of my calls! I had tried several accredited programs but I needed to have a high school diploma or a GED to get into them. Talk about being knocked down again and again.

I refused to be a statistic. I knew that an education was the way out so I went to a nearby technical college and obtained information on GED testing. They told me how much it cost and how to schedule them. After learning all of that, I scheduled my entire test for the following week. I purchased a GED book and refreshed myself by studying and reviewing things I wasn't sure about or couldn't remember.

The following week I went to the college to start my testing. I took my writing the first day, reading the second day, social studies the third day, science the fourth day and Math on the last day. I passed everything but the math test by a few points. I was a little disappointed but I was more determined to pass it.

I paid for another chance to take the math test and scheduled it but I failed it a second time by only five points. I decided that I needed to take a break to collect myself and reevaluate my options. I prayed and asked God to open up my understanding.

I was frustrated but in the meantime business had to be taken care of so I resumed taking body rub clients again. I only took regular clientele so there was no need to advertise.

I had previously went to school for medical assisting so I thought I'd try the medical field again.

I found a program to become a Certified Nurse Assistant (CNA) that was accredited. That course was only five weeks and under $1,000 so I jumped at the opportunity.

Home life was good and I was doing well with the body rubs. I had given up completely on any *funny business*. I had paid the first half of the tuition and began the CNA program.

I studied hard, went to school during the day and took a few clients after school. I was doing very well on tests, understanding the required procedures and the needed skill-set. Just when everything was going smoothly and I felt like I was gaining some momentum, this happened:

It started as a regular call to book an appointment so I set everything up as usual. When he arrived, I followed the same protocols as usual. We began the session and everything was going well. Toward the last 15 minutes of the session while I was doing some light feathering work on him, he forcefully grabbed my behind and began to put his mouth on me. I was startled, shocked and tried to get out of that awkward position. However, I started enjoying it so I gave in. I allowed him to finish performing this oral act.

Immediately after, I told Tae what had happened. I felt dirty, confused and didn't really understand what just took place. He had never done that before. He was always a cool client. Most of all, there was absolutely no attraction to him at all!

I was crying and upset. In that moment, I realized that it was deeper than I thought. All this time I thought that I could just stop because it was about the money. Clearly something else had happened along the way. I felt hopeless again like I had no control. I felt so bad that I didn't want to dance in the dance ministry anymore. I felt as though I had failed. I didn't know why I allowed it to happen.

I spoke to the dance ministry director and informed her that I could no longer be a part of the dance ministry. She asked me why and I told her all that had happened while sobbing uncontrollably. She told me that it was a tactic of the enemy and his goal was to get me to stop dancing. She encouraged me and told me that the conviction I was experiencing was a great sign and to follow it.

Later on, I decided that he would be my last client. I would not be taking anymore. I decided that that was going to be the last hiccup. I couldn't keep putting myself in the same situations while I was striving for change. I thought I needed what I was doing to get ahead so that I could get out that bad situation I was in but soon realized that I was going to have to put myself through school in a different way.

I decided to put all of my faith in God. Tae and I prayed to God for the finances to finish paying for my tuition. We believed that God would create a way. I continued to study hard and put in job applications like my life depended on it. Then we watched God supernaturally provide and bring finances in through favor and through Tae. I finished the program with a 3.9 GPA, receiving my certificate and license.

This win prompted me to go back and take the math portion of the GED test. I remember convincing myself that this would be the third and last time I would have to take that test because I was going to pass it. When I got the results, I was nervous but I passed. I was so excited! After all that I had been through as it pertains to my education, I finally obtained my GED and a license for a trade. The feeling was amazing!

My life was changing for the better. Our lease was coming to an end and we knew that we had to down size in order to make this new life work. I had accepted in my heart that living a life of luxury wasn't worth it. I had decided to give it all up so we moved to a townhouse where we continued to adjust our lives to those changes. It was rough for us financially.

I was trying to choose which part of the field I wanted to get into so I decided to take my certifications and work with children. I began to nanny professionally. That experience showed me the need for care with a standard that was affordable for families. So I decided to open my own in home care center.

Still remaining consistent in my pursuit of change and growth I got baptized. I had gained more spiritual clarity and knew that it was definitely time. I came up from the water feeling like a brand new woman.

During that time, I found out that my biological father was ill and had taken a turn for the worst. My sister Tammy and I still didn't get along and that situation just made it worst. Tammy and her husband came over to give me the update on how my dad was doing. I spoke to him over the phone but he was unable to speak to me because of how weak he was. I told my Dad how much I loved him and how I forgave him. I understood what happened to him. Then I prayed for him and asked him to make peace with God.

I don't remember exactly how but Tammy and I got into an awful argument. We were trying to make arrangements to go back home to see daddy but I was financially strapped. I had no money to contribute to get back home.

I was unable to see my dad one last time. I was unable to attend his funeral and I was unable to bury him. I know that my father understands why and is proud of the choices that I have made to be better but you could imagine the devastation I felt.

As time went on, we were unable to pay our rent because our car kept overheating. Finally we were faced with an eviction notice. We notified the parents that we were moving soon and that we would give them our new location shortly. I didn't like being in circumstances I couldn't control. I was used to being able to get us out of those types of problems. Tae comforted me and told me, "Because you gave up everything and sacrificed, he will always provide for you. You will never be without. Just continue to trust God."

We moved into a two bedroom apartment that was only a couple of miles away. We settled in and started up our home care center again. That home care center was successful for a few years. During that time, we taught the children basic curriculum including Spanish and sign language. We took the children on two trips per month; one of those trips was always to the library. I enjoyed making a difference in children's' lives. We worked closely with the children and their advancement was evident.

Our business grew because other parents would hear how well spoken and knowledgeable the children were so our popularity grew by word-of-mouth. I trained Tae so that the day care could keep running without me some of the time as I began working as a CNA to bring in more income. We were able to pay all of our bills with the income from my CNA work and our in home care center combined.

As we were approaching close to our third year of business, we decided to shut it down. We started to feel like some of the parents took advantage of our passion and love for the children. I decided to work as a CNA fulltime and Tae went back into the work force again.

I continued to go to church, serve on the dance ministry and had just joined the intercessory ministry. Then a thirst began to brew inside of me. One day after work, I went to my bedroom and got on the computer. Writing had always been therapeutic for me. As I typed out my thoughts everything in the room began to fall away.

All of a sudden, I was in a dessert. I could feel the sand beneath my feet. The sun was high and the heat was so real. I saw myself walking and complaining, "God why me? I'm not worthy. Find someone else. You must have made a mistake. You couldn't possibly use someone like me!"

Then I felt God's hand on my right shoulder. He calmly told me to "look."

The ground transformed from sand to this dry, baked looking dessert floor and the sun climbed even higher. There were chains coming out of the cracks of the ground. The people had chains on their ankles, wrists and necks. I was overcome with sorrow. I began to weep and say, "Lord help them! Why won't you help them? Don't you hear the cries of pain and agony?"

He said to me with his hand on my shoulder, "They are waiting to be offered living water; they are waiting for you."

I began to seek God in a way that was very different from the other times. My prayer life increased, fasting increased and intake of the word increased. In my sleep, I would hear someone calling me by name, over and over. When I woke up, it would still be dark outside. I'd look at my phone and it would be five in the morning. I laid back down and tried to go back to sleep. Again I heard "Robyn...Robyn" in the distance, as clear as day.

Finally, I said, "Holy Spirit, if it's you then please speak."

All I heard were the words "come away with me."

I got up and thanked God for his presence. Before I knew it, I was dancing before the Lord! There were times on the way home from work when I would rush into the house, turn on worship music and just dance before the Lord until I couldn't dance any more. It was like I couldn't hold it – like I had to offer it up to him!

I began to realize there was more to dancing in this way. It was like God was showing me how to come before him. One time, we were praying and worshipping in the house. The presence of God was so tangible that we quickly sat down. As we quieted ourselves, I was taken up!

All time stood still, I felt his love engulf me like a heavy winter blanket. The peace I felt was unimaginable. I just stayed there at his feet. I began to hear the Lord tell me, "It's time to go back."

I didn't want to, but I obeyed his command. I opened my eyes and Tae was lying on the living room floor, under the power of God!

The more I pursued him, the more I changed. At first, I didn't realize how much I was changing until everything around me also started to change. I recognized the change when my responses to these circumstances were completely different from what they would have been.

One morning I woke up and greeted the Father, Jesus and the Holy Spirit. I don't mean to come off as mystical but it was something I began to practice. On that particular morning after greeting the trinity, I began to worship and offer thanks. The Lord began to deal with me in a big way. He showed me the faces of different people; specifically those from my past who had hurt or harmed me.

As he showed me their faces, there was a download taking place within my spirit. With one person, I instantly knew why they did what they did as it pertained to me. With another person, it was acquired behavior and finally, another did it because of their insecurities. As the Lord showed me, he commanded that I make a confession.

I forgave my biological mom's boyfriend for molesting me. I understand that he was assigned by the enemy to plant a seed in my life at an early age. As the Lord revealed it, I confessed it. I sobbed a lot that morning but it was an intense release. I felt 15 pounds lighter. I felt like I had undergone brain surgery, like I had an intense spiritual therapy session. I had not only been renewed in my mind, but in my soul!

As time passed, the change continued. My mindset changed. My thought process surrounding certain things changed for the better. I continued to serve at church in the dance ministry, in the intercessors ministry and as a minister in training but I began to realize that opposition was coming from those that I had least expected! The leadership I respected and revered began to turn on me. Those incidents began to make going to church very uncomfortable. I couldn't understand why it was happening. The Leader I respected the most turned her back on me, mocked me, gossiped about me and even lied to others about me. It was so bad that when I would walk through the hallway and pass them they would just burst out laughing. I would greet some of the other members and they would just ignore me. Could you imagine wanting to defend yourself and speak your truth so bad but every time you fixed your lips the Holy Spirit arrested you. The whole situation depressed me- I just cried and cried. It made my partner very upset to see what all was happening.

The very thing I cherished the most was turning its back on me. Whatever it was that caused them to act this way towards me is still very unclear however I had heard rumors one was that I was trying to take the leadership position. My response was always that couldn't be it because they know me. I learned quickly not everyone takes the time to discern and learn those they labor among. This is one of the quickest ways the enemy infiltrates ministries and easily divides. There was so much happening that it broke my heart. Going through all this pushed me even closer to God. I'm grateful that it happened- it pushed this little eaglet right out of the nest, it was time for me to soar. Had it never happened I would have just kept serving and would of never had time for what God had chosen me to birth.

During that time, I worked as a CNA. It was a time of spiritual growth for me. While I was on a 44 day fast, seeking and prayer journey, the Lord reminded me of the vision he gave me in the desert – reminding me of those waiting on me!

During that time, I received the download for Heart Of A D.I.V.A Ministries. That ministry traveled all over, teaching and imparting into others what the Lord had shown me. Simply put, that was how to go before him using dance. It became so unbearable at church that I finally left! If those things would have never happened to me, I reiterate I would have stayed in my comfort zone serving with joy. It wasn't until these uncomfortable instances happened that I was forced to leave the nest.

Toward the end of the 44 day fast, the Lord specifically commissioned me to "restore the balance" in the spiritual dance. People either had technique or were not a carrier of his presence or they had an awesome relationship with God, carrying His presence but lacked technique. It was my assignment to teach and show those in pursuit how to bring both forth both through movement. I was to teach them that technique wasn't limited to actual dance vocabulary or classical movement. They needed to practice in order to bring clear, defined movement. That way, those watching could understand the message being shared.

Heart Of A D.I.VA was in existence for about eight months and had successfully facilitated a summer camp, several classes, workshops and started a dance company. We had our first official interview when I decided that I wanted to study even more. I ended up joining this international network for dance ministers where the founder offered courses. That's where I got my Liturgical Dance Teacher certificate! The course was confirming for me since a lot of the material I knew through what the Lord had shown me. It was fascinating to receive so much confirmation.

However, there were also a lot of things that I didn't know so I still studied hard. I graduated from the program and was given the opportunity to meet build friendships with people that were like-minded.

As time went on, the founder of the network reached out to me and I began to serve. I would take her to events or help drive to events. I was somewhat like an assistant. Everything was fine until I received a phone call from her asking about my personal life. Who I was in a relationship with, how long we had been together and why I never told her anything about my girlfriend.

I had apologized to her if she felt that there was any deception. I said that I wanted my fruit to speak for itself. I explained to her that who I am with didn't define me as a person. My identity was in Jesus Christ! I went on to remind her that she had spent time with me and I asked her, "Did you not discern my spirit and my heart for God?"

She said to me, "Gifts are without repentance."

I was to worship God in spirit and in truth. The whole time I cried uncontrollably on the phone.

I had experienced hurt from those in power before but that time it felt like someone shot me in my heart. I went into depression, argued with Tae and eventually broke up with her. I was confused and in pain every day. I had sent an email asking her for a list of churches but got no answer. I sent another email asking for a list of places I could go, informing her that I was leaving and how I had broken it off with Tae. I still got no answer.

I called her a week or two after and told her that I thought it was best to just remove myself from serving in her organization. It was not my intention to hurt or shame anyone. She said that she had been doing some thinking and praying herself and that she agreed. It was best that I leave!

I continued to go through each day, even though I was broken down. I cried and prayed a lot during that time.

I cried out, "Lord you have delivered me from so much. How is it you won't deliver me from this? If this is sin in your sight then where is the way of escape you promised? Why would you call me to do your work just to make mockery of me?"

I couldn't understand it. After a while, I realized that this Pastor never prayed for me so that I could get "delivered." I realized she was more concerned about her image and what would happen to her brand if people found out that I was connected to her. She could care less about my soul. That was the same Pastor who went to my home church gala event to accept an award. I also realized that I was worshipping God in spirit and truth. I was bold enough to give him all of me. I withheld nothing. He knew me and I knew him! After going through that, the Lord told me to go back to church. My sabbatical was over.

The Lord charged me going forward that when I was asked any questions in regards to that, to walk in integrity. I was to let it be known and to give that information when I was led by his spirit to do so. The whole time, being in a relationship with Tae was never a big deal for me until I started moving out in the "ministry." Then I realized that not everyone believed what I believed.

It's sad to say that I experienced this confusion more than once. It was confusion on my part for several reasons.

For one, Tae was the first and only relationship I had been in. I was unsure what that meant for me, my sexuality and how I saw myself. Was I okay with myself? Prior to her, I had always dated and been with men.

Secondly, I had a relationship with God and I was sensitive to his spirit. I never felt conviction for being with her.

Thirdly, I had experienced the power of God – the kind of power that we rarely see in our churches today. I had encountered him in more ways than this book has shown. Not once was my being with a woman ever an issue with him.

However, I was tormented by the thought of what people would think of me and what they would say about me. I was afraid of them finding out I was with a woman and how that would change everything. It amazed me how I was the most anointed person to ever grace their stage or pulpit to this person that needed deliverance from demonic spirits. I watched leaders prophecy me to the nations, calling me a prophet, anointed and a giant in the Kingdom of God even and then shun me.

It's either I hear from God or I don't; it's either I'm anointed or I'm not. Going through this continually cause me to mourn myself into spells of depression. I was so heavily conflicted. There were times when I would fast and ask God to make away if I wasn't in his will or to send the help I needed to get out of the relationship.

However, I did have one positive experience. Heart Of A D.I.V.A hosted a workshop and a lady came from another state to be a part of it. She said that she enjoyed the presence of God so much that she wanted to go to church with us on that Sunday. I explained to her that we typically rest after pouring out like that so I wouldn't be at church on Sunday. I gave her a short list of churches in the area. She said that she was going to go to our church; she didn't need the list.

That night I tossed and turned a lot. All I could hear was the Holy Spirit tell me to "go to church" over and over throughout the night. I sprung up that morning and got ready for church. At church when it was time to welcome the visitors, that lady was among them.

I began to sweat so much that you could see the print in my blouse. I was prompted to have her sit with me for the service. I walked her to the restroom and asked her what her thoughts were. I told her that my church was different in the sense that we welcomed **ALL** people. We believed the gospel of Jesus Christ was for everyone and we didn't believe in exclusion. The love of Christ was for all people.

She replied, "Yes. I did notice that."

At the end of the service, I took her to meet the Pastor and then saw her off. I asked her if she enjoyed the service and she said that she did enjoy it.

A week went by and nothing happened at the start of the following week, she called me and said, "Robyn, since I have been back home I have shared my experience with my husband and have been deep in prayer. I'm going to be honest with you. At first, I was confused. I have been walking with the Lord for a long time and I know him.

At your workshop, there was no doubt that the presence of God and demonstration of his Kingdom was there. When I first got to your church and realized there were gay people there, I told myself that 'God is about to strike this place down with fire!' They are all going to hell. Then I realized that I was in a room full of people who wanted Jesus and loved him just like I do. The word was good and the worship experience was beautiful.

I felt the presence of God there as well. You can see how this had me baffled and that's when my husband suggested that we pray.

I may not ever understand it but the one thing I know is that I am supposed to love. I don't have a hell to put anyone in! The Lord dealt with me and asked me who I thought I was. I just want to let you know that because of this experience, I am going to write a book and I want your permission to use you as one of my examples."

I was completely blown away. All I could do was cry and say "thank you."

I then went on to say while tears streamed down my face, Could you imagine someone saying Jesus didn't love you because you were in a same gendered relationship?"

I thanked her again for her honesty and for seeing me as God saw me.

Even after that experience, I would still battle bouts of depression because of the lack of inner peace. I was torn between what I was taught, what others said and the fear of God being ashamed of me. There were times I fasted and prayed, begging God to tell me if I was in error or had shamed him because of my relationship.

There were times when I became angry with God because I couldn't understand why the same God that delivered me had become silent. I was confused. How was it that the same God who delivered me left the desire to stay in a relationship with a woman behind if it were wrong?

I had to go through a process. I began to study the word more for myself and my findings were surprising. I realized that I had nothing to prove to people. I wasn't living for them. I was living for Christ! My life was and is an example of his grace and saving power. That's all that mattered.

The process wasn't an easy one. It's one thing to say you are free from people but it's quite another thing to actually be free of them. It's only natural to want to be accepted by your peers and loved ones. I had never fit in my whole life; I was always different and often misunderstood. People are people. They will judge and gossip no matter what you do so I made the decision to be happy and not put energy into things that I couldn't change.

I have watched God move all over my life. Not only did he deliver me from adult entertainment, alcoholism and smoking, but he also healed the relationships in my family. My sister Tammy and I are closer than ever. My mother and I now have an understanding. We have learned how to love, respect and cherish one another despite the things we may not agree on. Most of all, we have forgiven one another.

I experienced deliverance from soul ties, promiscuity, the desire for that type of attention and the need to fulfill the desires of my members in that way. My mind had been renewed and freed! Freed from those thought patterns and systems that would cause me to see people as dollar signs, distort what real relationships are like, to think that the glamour of that industry is real and the belief that I wasn't in slavery. My mind was so far gone that I can't begin to list all the things I had received deliverance from.

My heart and soul received tremendous healing! I didn't realize it until one year later when my Mom Raven came down for Thanksgiving (my favorite holiday of the year). We all ate, talked and laughed. My sister Tammy suggested that I dance for the family. So I put on the music and started to dance before the Lord. There was a hush that came over the house. Some of my family members began to weep silently; the tears just fell. My Mother got up and went outside, weeping uncontrollably. She began to say how faithful God was and how proud she was of me. She went on to apologize for when I was younger. Something rose up on the inside of me. Instead of soaking in the moment that I had I waited for my whole life, I began to minister to my mom and tell her that it was time to let go of the guilt and shame. I told her that she was free and that it was time for her to receive her healing!

That night I told Tae what happened in astonishment. I told her I had been waiting for that moment my whole life, how I dreamed of what I would say and how I would just let her have it once and for all, but instead I ministered to her. I knew right in that moment that my heart had been changed for real! I had received a new heart and God was surely healing my soul from the traumas that I had experienced.

I suffered with anger issues that would cause me to lash out. I am still in the process of changing (trying not to go from 0 to 100) but I am so much better in the way I handle things and those closest to me. Being able to uncover some of the roots and triggers to my anger has helped so much. I have also experienced healing from some of the things that used to trigger an episode. I can't remember the last time I had a flash back.

I got to a place in my life where I decided to take therapy. I wanted to make sure that nothing gets over-looked. I went from hating therapy as a child to loving it as an adult. I realized that I have nothing to be ashamed of. What's important to me is to be completely whole in every area and aspect of my life. My partner Tae and I also do therapy sessions together as we are still healing certain areas of our relationship from the trauma we had experienced together in the past. We are engaged and can't wait to continue to spend the rest of our lives together and build together.

I'm not sure why it took me so long to arrive at this place as we have been together for 7 years. Maybe I was just afraid of marriage and that level of commitment being that I had never really saw a healthy relationship or marriage up close before and wanted to save myself from what I thought was inevitable. Whatever my hang ups were I decided that I deserved to be happy and Tae makes me happy. No one can answer to God for me but me! People may not agree or even believe that God is in the mist of us, our union and or even abiding in us let alone using us (Tae and I). However I assure you that our Lord and Savior is ever so present in our lives together as well as individually.

I am grateful today because I am **FREE**! I am who God created me to be – nothing more, nothing less. He has liberated me through his gift of salvation and constant process of sanctification. My life experiences have enabled me to continue empowering others. I can be a voice for the silent. I can't afford to give up when others are in need. I don't know what the future holds. The pages of my life are still being written as I continue to walk with the Lord. One thing that is for certain is that I went...

From the Pole to fulfilling Prophesy...

From an Escort to an Exhorter...

From a Mistress to a Minister...

From a Stripper to a Speaker...

From an Adult entertainer to an Author!

"If the Son therefore shall make you free, ye shall be free indeed."

~ John 8:36 KJV

"For God so loved the world that he gave his only begotten Son, that whosoever believeth in him should not perish, but have everlasting life."

~ John 3:16 KJV

Illusions of Glamour & Grandeur Initiative

Illusions of Glamour and Grandeur is an initiative by Triumph Multi-National Inc. that brings awareness about the world of adult entertainment and the sex industry. Our goal is to provide intervention and prevention by way of partnering with others for our social media campaign to spread the naked truth about this industry and the harm it causes. Our Campaign has 3 phases (The Glamour & Grandeur, Statistics & Truth, and Testimonies of Triumph). Our outreach consists of speaking at different events and places to raise awareness in hopes to prevent and by going back into those very places to pull women out! Each woman that contacts Triumph Multi-National Inc. receives one of our Triumphant Jewels Care packages with resources that will help assist them on their way out the industry and to help build their faith. All care packages support and services are free of Charge for the women.

How you can Help:

- Partner with us so we can make a greater impact (by volunteering, sharing your story for the campaign, reoccurring monthly donations, donate your professional services and or donate gifts in kind such as cosmetics and perfumes for our outreach bags)
- Purchase this book as a gift for women in shelters, crisis centers, colleges, residential programs, prisons and any other places you think people will be encouraged and or

empowered.

- Make a one- time monetary contribution online.
- Invite Robyn out to speak at your organization or upcoming Event. Our website www.triumphmultinational.org

About Triumph Multi-National Inc.

Triumph Multi-National Inc. is a faith based non-profit organization for girls and women ages 12-Adult with a radical non-traditional approach. Our vision is to be a multi-national international oasis and safe haven of empowerment and restoration for girls and women worldwide, no matter their background, walk of life and or current conditions. Our mission is to serve, restore, liberate, empower and equip ***"the whole"*** girl and woman by offering services, programs, professional and spiritual assistance through counseling/solution sessions, training, retreats, camps, conferences, workshops and tele-seminars- all to assist each girl and or woman towards their goal. T.R.I.U.M.P.H is an acronym for Truth Revealed In U Manifested Purpose Him

In every girl and woman there is potential, purpose and destiny that sometimes lies dormant , covered by the traumatic experiences life may have thrown your way until it is realized, awakened and or utilized. The question then becomes; how do I overcome to be able to access what's on the inside of me? How do I utilize it to my advantage? Well once the **T**ruth is **R**evealed **I**n **U**, you will realize that, that truth is your **M**anifested **P**urpose in **H**im and it's only the beginning! Join us on this Journey as we empower you to Live Life Everyday Triumphant!

Looking to Get out of the Adult Entertainment Industry?

No matter what part of the industry you were in there is help. On the next page you will find some organizations to help you begin your new journey! Seize this opportunity, take this moment and make a decision that will help you realize your purpose so that you can begin to walk out destiny! It's not too late!

The first step into your new journey is the acceptance of Jesus Christ as your Lord and Savior into your heart. You won't be able to conquer this alone! If you are tired of the darkness, vicious cycles, those feelings of emptiness, pain and anger or the reoccurring feelings of being unloved, rejected, unwanted and or worthlessness. I want you to know that God sees you and thinks that you are beautiful, handsome and that there is nothing to dirty that you could ever do that would stop Him from loving you and embracing you.

That's what I love about God, He is not like mankind! His love is truly unconditional and he is there with you right now, with his arms stretched wide ready and waiting to receive you. If you want to you can receive this kind of love right now! This love will cleanse you and erase the shame, this love will give you beauty for ashes and this love has been waiting just for you. ***Just say this prayer out loud as you read it:***

God I confess that I am a sinner. I ask that you forgive me of all my sins. I believe in my heart that your son Jesus Christ was God in the flesh, I believe He died on the cross for all of my sins. I believe that on the 3rd day He rose with all power and that he is alive today. I believe that he conquered sin, hell and the grave for me. Lord Jesus I ask that you come into my heart, I ask that you save me, help me, heal me, deliver me and release your love in me and on my life. I ask that you become my Lord and Master in my heart and over my life. By this confession of belief I am saved!

My Prayer for You:

Lord I ask that as a sign of your love for them that you begin to touch right now releasing your love let your love intensify as they continue to read this prayer! Lord keep each and every person that made the choice to receive you in their hearts. I thank you that they will begin to see themselves the way you see them. I thank you that no weapon formed against them shall prosper. I thank you that you will give them a hunger and thirst for you that no man can put out. I thank you that you will provide every need according to your riches and glory. I thank you that every lie and evil seed the enemy told or planted is consumed by your fire. I thank you that you are breaking every illegal soul tie and that you are healing and renewing their souls. I thank you for the renewing of their minds and the adjustment of perspectives and thought patterns.

I thank you that every system in which they once operated in now becomes the systems of our Lord Jesus Christ. I thank you that you purge and send your consuming fire to consume everything that is not like you as well as anything that will hinder, sabotage and block them emotionally, physically, mentally, spiritually, relationally and economically. Restore unto them and redeem their time, give them Hines feet that they may be steadfast in you and on the decision that they have made today. Commune with them giving them divine life changing encounters; release your peace and love upon them daily.

In Jesus Mighty, Matchless Name- Amen!!

Looking to Get Out of the Adult Entertainment Industry?

Here is some help!

Triumph Multi-National Inc.
www.triumphmultinational.org

Pink Cross Foundation
www.thepinkcross.org

Beauty from Ashes Ministries, Inc.
www.beautyfromashes.org

Way Out
www.onewayout.org

4Sarah
www.4sarah.net

Hookers for Jesus
www.hookersforjesus.net

Excerpt From The Upcoming Book

"Are They ALL Dead Yet?"

As I lay on the bed starring off in to space thinking of the dream I had the night before. A clear calm voice simply asked are they all dead yet??? I immediately began to think of what that could possibly mean. Then in an instance I suddenly realized that every persona I had created while in the adult entertainment industry had a strong man in which enabled me to operate as such.

I also thought to myself the old me is completely dead, I believe I have been fully delivered. Then I remembered that when God poses a question it's not that He doesn't know the answer. It's that He wants us to arrive at the same understanding which in turn gives us the answer.

I began to review and play things back in my head and after a short period of time. I realized the answer was simply no. There was no need to sugar coat it because the Almighty already knows all. He only asked to make me aware of my current spiritual state.

It wasn't that I was a bad person, I wasn't possessed but there were clearly some things he wanted me to know. Like the ones that were still attached to me lying dormant waiting for the perfect opportunity to attack. Or those that wait patiently for the anniversary to come knocking to see if you are weak enough to let it and 7 more in. Since my thirst was never quenched I was not satisfied and continued my pursuit of Him.

I soon realized that the type of deliverance I needed had to take place in my soul. In the dream the night before the demon looked at my chest and said "I'll be back".

Pondering all these things began to drive me up the wall. So I prayed for sight, insight, understanding and wisdom. I would soon find out that the Spirit of the Lord would give me more than what I asked for. He showed me things, specific things, entry ways, the way they operate, and their functions.

What am I talking about exactly? I'm glad that you asked. I'm talking about the realm of the spirit, specifically the forces of darkness. Demonic or evil forces if you will. Yes my friend that realm is very real. As I submitted to yet another process of deliverance the Lord revealed to me what I will share with you in this book.

Some you have heard of, some may have even been preached or taught on but then there are those you rarely hear about. I call those demons silent killers. You can't defeat something you don't know exist! The enemy is very strategic and has a way about doing things.

"My people are destroyed for lack of knowledge......."

~ ***Hosea 4:6 KJV***

Through this book we will reveal and or show you how these demonic forces entered my life, operated in my life through adult entertainment, life experiences and trauma. This book will empower you to recognize and know when these forces are present and or at work. It is my prayer that this knowledge empowers you in such a way that you may be used by God to help deliver others!

Excerpt From The Upcoming Book

"Daddy's Little Girl: Daughters of God"

What does a daughter of God look like? I asked myself..... Well she must be virtuous, humble, gentle, loving, displaying all the fruits of the Spirit! Then I pictured Mother Theresa and thought surely she wasn't perfect, she had to have something that she was constantly in prayer about.

Then I thought a good daughter never changes position, she never leaves where she is at without the direction of her father. She trusts her father and she knows her father. Well what does this mean for us? It means that we are not expected to be perfect but we are expected to be whole and obedient! When the Lord has positioned us, we want Him to find us where He left us. The Lord should never ever have to look for us once we have reached maturity. As a child we would wonder off but as an adolescent we've come to know better. So what am I saying? I'm saying that we want to perfect the discipline of "being still & waiting in the Lord!"

This discipline is a hard one, one that I have missed many times. I pay the price every time I forget to be still. A wise woman once told me "If the Lord is saying nothing, do nothing" – Remain in that same position. I've come to learn that in order to perfect the discipline of being still and waiting in the Lord you must be obedient and be unmovable in discomfort. One of my silent prayers has always been: "Lord help me to have extreme obedience, I want to obey you blindly like Abraham did!

See as children our parents have always guided us by giving us instructions and structure. We may have not understood why but we obeyed. The times we didn't obey there was what it seemed to be 2 sets of consequences. The first being the ***natural*** consequence, the law of cause and effect, for ex:

Mom: "Don't touch the stove Leslie!

When Mom wasn't looking Leslie touch the stove, immediately she suffered a burn on her hand. As you can see here the first consequence was the natural occurrence of cause and affect due to disobedience; Leslie hand was burned and she experienced pain. The second consequence ex 2: *Leslie begins to cry out and weep. Mom came to the rescue and cared for her daughters burns. After Mom patched her up she began to verbally discipline Leslie and she was sent to her room to think about what she had done.*

Here we see that after being burned, Leslie still had to face what she had done which was disobeying her mother's instructions. She received verbal reprimand and was sent to her room. So we can conclude that the second consequence were the ones given by her Mom, her guardian, her caregiver.

See the Lord God is not a respecter of persons but of laws, principles and systems. Our Lord does not change the laws that He has created and put in place just to excuse us. As our Father He desires to protect, provide, love and care for us. When He gives instructions or guidelines they are for our own good and protection. He sees all, knows all and desires to keep us. Like our natural parents He wants the best for us. So we must learn to obey even when we don't understand. I used to think God was a little like a tyrant because I felt as though I couldn't do anything! As life went on and I experienced hurt, pain, bitterness, rejection and more. I began to understand more clearly the importance of having and following the Father's instructions and guidelines. I then developed an appreciation for His wisdom and realized His love is amazing. As daughters of God we must learn and walk in "Blind Obedience" and have the spiritual maturity to accept the set of consequences that come with disobedience, repenting and thanking God for His grace and mercy which abides through Jesus Christ!

Paul says it best

"What then? shall we sin, because we are not under the law, but under grace? God forbid."

~ Romans 6:15 KJV

Just because our Father gives us grace let us not take it for granted but strive to have "Blind Obedience."

"And Samuel said, Hath the Lord as great delight in burnt offerings and sacrifices, as in obeying the voice of the Lord? Behold, to obey is better than sacrifice, and to hearken than the fat of rams."

~ 1 Samuel 15:22 KJV

Let us begin this journey of healing. Together we will heal the little girl within, break free of our dysfunctions and past experiences. We will discover the process and benefits of servant hood to daughtership to the King of Kings! It's time to live life everyday triumphant!

ABOUT THE AUTHOR

Robyn Robbins is an Author, Entrepreneur, Speaker and Visionary. She is the Founder of Heart Of A D.I.V.A Ministries LLC and all of its extensions. She is President of Triumph Multi-National Inc. and CEO of Robyn Robbins Enterprises. Her goal is to simply enrich, empower and liberate ALL that cross her path! She is no stranger to the grace, mercy and delivering power, in which we receive through Jesus Christ; as God saw fit to save her life, cultivate her using her passion and gift of dance in order to catapult her into the calling and destiny that He preordained.

It is her ultimate desire to design a comprehensive program for broken, battered women and those who desire to leave the adult entertainment world. This program will rehabilitate and give the help that's needed and truly required to start over.

"God is a God of many chances!" She exclaims "it's only right that we extend that same love and grace to those in need." In Robyn's spare time she enjoys music, the arts and the many facets of expression. She adores chic, edgy forward fashion and make-up. She loves being surrounded by family, close friends, a great meal and a good glass of red wine. Robyn loves to empower and motivate others to turn aspirations into reality, to realize and birth their dreams and teaching how to turn your passions, talents and gifts into business. She enjoys soaking and receiving revelatory downloads in the presence of God.

Connect with Me Beyond the Book

Social Media Platforms:

www.Facebook.com/robynrobbinsenterprises

www.instagram.com/robynrobbinsenterprises

Twitter & Blab : @ robynrobbinsent

Periscope: @robynrobbins

Book Robyn To Speak:

Robyn has crafted powerful, eye opening and liberating talks that derived from this book that offers the attendee an experience. Such as "Loving the Authentic You", "Finding the road to freedom" and "Flipping your Street Savvy". To book her for one of these talks or to simply share her story send inquires to info@robynrobbins.com or call 1-888-637-1277 ext 3, for more detailed information go to www.robynrobbins.com.

Bulk Order Information:

Discounts are available on quantity orders from corporations, organizations, associations and others. Contact info@robynrobbins.com for more information on bulk orders.

Orders for wholesalers and U.S. trade bookstores contact information is the same displayed above

Are You an Aspiring Author, A beginner in Authorship or even a Pro?

Do you have a story that the world needs to hear? Are you looking to inspire and empower others with words? Are you looking for opportunities to make self publishing easier but you aren't sure how? Are you tired of scrambling around to put your book together in excellence? Maybe you are just starting out and you are unsure of where exactly to start. Your days of worry are over today my friend. Yes! Now there is a place that has been created with authors in mind to assist you on your journey and the great thing about it is that it's all in one place.

Yes my friend you heard me correctly it's all in one place. Everything an author needs to birth a book! I have had the honor to become a representative for such a company and contribute by offering consultations. Yes, I'm kind of like your cheerleader and coach wrapped all in one. I'll hold your hand and walk you through the process until your baby (book) is born. Check out the info below, we can't wait to serve you!

Sources

The Authors Help Desk TM

The Holy Bible

www.Google.com (assistance for adult entertainers)

Diaries of An Ex-Adult Entertainer: My Road to Redemption

This is My Life, My Journey, My Story, My Testimony

An Autobiography

53790598R00084

Made in the USA
Charleston, SC
18 March 2016